Organize Your

Family's Schedule

...In No Time

Valentina Sgro

800 East 96th Street,
Indianapolis, Indiana 46240

Organize Your Family's Schedule In No Time

Copyright © 2005 by Que

International Standard Book Number: 0-7897-3220-3

Library of Congress Catalog Card Number: 2004107645

Printed in the United States of America

First Printing: October 2004

07   06   05   04   4   3   2

Trademarks

Warning and Disclaimer

Bulk Sales

Que offers excellent discounts on this book when ordered in quantity for bulk purchases or special sales. For more information, please contact

U.S. Corporate and Government Sales
1-800-382-3419
corpsales@pearsontechgroup.com

For sales outside the United States, please contact

International Sales
international@pearsoned.com

Executive Editor
Candace Hall

Development Editor
Lorna Gentry

Managing Editor
Charlotte Clapp

Project Editor
Tonya Simpson

Copy Editor
Charles A. Hutchinson

Indexer
Ken Johnson

Proofreader
Eileen Dennie

Technical Editor
Ann Gambrell

Publishing Coordinator
Cindy Teeters

Designer
Anne Jones

Cover Illustrator
Nathan Clement, Stickman Studio

Page Layout
Bronkella Publishing

Table of Contents

I The Mechanics of Family Scheduling– Tools and Techniques

5 Celebrating Special Occasions................................**97**

Scheduling Family Celebrations 98
    Putting Important Dates on Your Family's Calendar 98
    Setting Aside Enough Time to Celebrate 99
    Planning 99
    Preparing 102
    Celebrating 107
    Preserving the Memories 107

Planning Your Holidays 108
    Choosing the Holidays You'll Celebrate 109
    Incorporating the Holidays into Your Family's Schedule 109

Keeping (or Losing) Family Traditions 110

Chapter Summary 112

6 Participating in Enrichment Activities................................**113**

Deciding How to Spend Your Time 114
    Analyzing Your Options 114
    Sorting Out Your Preferences 117

Avoiding Scheduling Conflicts 120
    Choosing Between Overlapping Activities 121
    Scheduling Drivers, Spectators, and Other Family Participants 122
    Resolving Conflicts with Other Family Events and Activities 122

Applying the Basics 125
    Scheduling All Phases of the Activity 126
    Setting Up Systems to Save Time 127
    Periodically Reevaluating Enrichment Activity Schedules 129

Chapter Summary 130

7 Planning Other Fun Stuff................................**131**

Family Vacations 132
    Before You Go 132
    While You're There 136
    Upon Your Return 136

Hobbies 137

Socializing 138

III Scheduling for All of Your Family Members

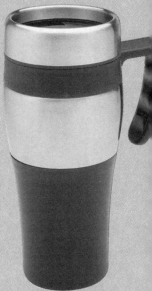

IV Appendixes

About the Author

In 1985, Valentina Sgro left her 12-hour-a-day position at a major law firm for a 16-hour-a-day job of childrearing and household management. In 1989, realizing that things were out of control, Val began trying to find a system that would get her organized. In 1997, with order established in her own life, Val founded SGRO Consulting, Solutions for Getting *Really* Organized.

Val consults privately and lectures regularly on various organizing topics. She writes a monthly article for the SGRO Consulting website: www.ReallyOrganized.com.

Val is a Chronic Disorganization Specialist and a member of the Golden Circle of the National Association of Professional Organizers (NAPO). She is serving in her third year on NAPO's board of directors, currently as its treasurer. Val also is a past treasurer of the National Study Group on Chronic Disorganization (NSGCD).

Val enjoys sharing her increased productivity and free time with her husband and their son.

Dedication

This book is dedicated to my family:

My parents Albert J. and Frances M.G. Sgro

My husband Carl E. Cormany

and

My son Edward Sgro Cormany

Acknowledgments

Many people have contributed to this book in many ways, and I realize that the more people I name, the more likely I'll be to leave someone out. My sincere thanks truly go to everyone who helped in any way with any aspect of my life, career, or writing which has led to the creation of this book.

I do want to thank publicly a handful of very special people:

Carl Cormany, my husband, for his incredible support and encouragement and his in-house editorial and proofreading skills;

Ed Cormany, my son, for both his encouragement and his technical help with creating this book's graphics;

Lily Rose, my goddaughter; Joey Rose, one of her brothers; and Leslie Caplan, my lifelong friend, for their ideas and insights on family dynamics, which I've used in this book; and

Barry Izsak, my professional organizing colleague and friend, for being a patient inspiriter throughout my writing of this book.

We Want to Hear from You!

As the reader of this book, *you* are our most important critic and commentator. We value your opinion and want to know what we're doing right, what we could do better, what areas you'd like to see us publish in, and any other words of wisdom you're willing to pass our way.

As an executive editor for Que, I welcome your comments. You can email or write me directly to let me know what you did or didn't like about this book—as well as what we can do to make our books better.

Please note that I cannot help you with technical problems related to the topic of this book. We do have a User Services group, however, where I will forward specific technical questions related to the book.

When you write, please be sure to include this book's title and author as well as your name, email address, and phone number. I will carefully review your comments and share them with the author and editors who worked on the book.

Email: feedback@quepublishing.com

Mail: Candace Hall
Executive Editor
Que Publishing
800 East 96th Street
Indianapolis, IN 46240 USA

For more information about this book or another Que Publishing title, visit our website at www.quepublishing.com. Type the ISBN (excluding hyphens) or the title of a book in the Search field to find the page you're looking for.

Introduction

"Too much to do; too little time." If this phrase expresses how you feel, you are not alone, and this book is for you!

Family schedules get out of control for various reasons. In one instance, they may start off simple and continue to have things added to them with no particular plan; this type of schedule is inefficient from the beginning, but you realize it only after you've added so many activities that you aren't accomplishing them all. In another instance, someone makes a real attempt to plan everything so it will work well, but the tools selected don't match the needs of the family, so they fall into disuse and the schedule deteriorates. This book addresses your scheduling problem at its cause and will show you how to simply and easily organize your family's schedule without upsetting your family's planned activities in the meantime.

What This Book Can Do for You

The *In No Time* series of books is designed to take a step-by-step approach to guiding you to accomplish your goal. The books contain lots of to do lists so that you don't have to spend a lot of time reading through theory and then trying to figure out what you actually need to do. This book won't take you a long time to read, and, at the end, you'll see practical results.

Many books cover principles of time management: how to set goals, prioritize tasks, and get more work done in less time. And many books tell you how to organize your home and office: how to reduce clutter, process paperwork, and store possessions. This book, on the other hand, takes the unique approach of concentrating on how to organize your family's schedule: how to take the complex mix of jobs, chores, events, and activities of all of your family members and arrange them so that everything gets done without a mad scramble by anyone.

This book does not try to tell you the one "right" system to use. Instead, we'll take you through a series of self-evaluations that will guide you to selecting a system that will complement the individual personalities and interests of your family members. After you've selected the system that's appropriate for your family, then we'll show you how to use it, and you can disregard the material explaining the other systems.

Regardless of the system you select, if you follow the steps in this easy-to-read book, you'll have your family's schedule arranged so that

- All of your family members are comfortable with the planner system you're using, because you'll have selected a main planner and supplemental planning tools that work well with your family members' individual styles.
- All of your family members are satisfied with what they're expected or allowed to do, because you'll have designed the schedule fairly, taking into account each person's preferences and distributing the burdens and benefits— okay, call it the work and the play—equitably.
- Your family's life runs smoothly with a lot less stress, because you've loosened up the scheduling by eliminating some unnecessary activities, streamlining some required chores, and adding some more fun events.
- You function as a coordinated family, rather than a group of individuals running in different directions, because you've made the small investment of time needed to align all of the components.

Who Should Read This Book?

It doesn't matter if you have a young family or one in which the kids are almost grown, if you have a family with just one child or a dozen children, or if you avoid technology or embrace it; this book is for you if

- You're finding it difficult to coordinate your family members' schedules
- You want your family to be able to do more with less stress

- You don't understand why your family members can't follow a schedule even when they've agreed to it
- You think you're so busy that you don't have time to organize your family's schedule

Or, you might want to use this book if you're in the process of combining two households and want to get your joint venture off and running smoothly. In fact, you may even want to read this book if you're just starting a family, because while we've made it easy to get your family's out-of-control schedule organized, it's always easier if you start off organized instead.

How This Book Is Organized

To help you focus in on exactly what you need, we've divided this book into three main parts.

Part I, "The Mechanics of Family Scheduling—Tools and Techniques," explains the tools and techniques you'll need to establish and maintain a smooth-running family schedule. We'll take you on a tour of the many calendars, planners, and schedulers—both hard copy and electronic—that are available. Plus, we'll give you simple questionnaires to help you choose the tools that are best for your family. Then we'll show you how to set up your system and get your family involved using it.

Part II, "Life's Activities," divides the items your family needs to schedule by categories: necessities, celebrations, enrichment activities, and leisure time. We'll show you how to make sure you have ample time for each area.

Part III, "Scheduling for All Your Family Members," explores how family scheduling is different depending on the ages of the family members. We'll focus on scheduling issues that are unique to each age group: preschoolers, school-age children, teenagers, parents, and senior citizens. We'll show you how to make sure that no one group takes over or is left out.

How to Use This Book

You're welcome to read this book from cover to cover, of course, but what we really want you to do is to use this book to improve your family's life.

In Chapter 1, "Selecting a Planner," we'll help you decide whether to use a hardcopy or electronic system. So, it makes sense that when you get to Chapter 2, "Setting Up Your Planner," you'll need to read only the sections that apply to the type of system you'll be using. On the other hand, you'll notice we recommend that you hold off making your final decision until you've read all of the sections of the book that apply to you, so you may want to read about how to set up both types of systems, because what you learn may influence your final decision.

In addition, each chapter in Parts II and III of this book is a self-contained unit of information, so if a certain topic doesn't apply to your family—for example, if you don't have any preschoolers—then there's no need for you to spend time on that chapter.

Special Elements and Icons

We've done our best to arrange the material in this book so that you can zero in on what you need. So, we've added some special elements to help you spot information:

- Many sections begin with a *Things You'll Need* list. This list will let you know whether you should have any supplies on hand as you read the section. If you have what you need as you read the chapter, you can complete the recommended steps right away, and you won't have to come back to do them later.

- For major projects, we've provided you with *timelines* that will help you get all of the tasks into your schedule at the appropriate times.

- We've set aside some information as *tips*. Tips indicate fairly easy actions you can take that will have a large, positive impact on your schedule.

- On the other hand, we've flagged other information as *cautions*. Cautions don't talk about worst-case scenarios; they indicate negative results that are likely to occur if you don't guard against them.

- *Notes* give you little tidbits of interesting information about the topic we're discussing in the main body of text.

- At the end of each chapter, you'll find a *Chapter Checklist* that you can use to make sure you've done everything necessary to accomplish the goals outlined at the beginning of the chapter in the *In This Chapter* list.

We've also flagged four particular types of information with special icons:

- The *Brain Wave* icon indicates material that gives you insight into how people think. It may be information on different learning and functioning modalities and the types of scheduling tools that work better for each of them. Or it may be a layman's explanation of psychological or emotional factors that may influence a person's tendency to accept or reject a certain type of scheduling.

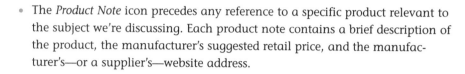

- The *Product Note* icon precedes any reference to a specific product relevant to the subject we're discussing. Each product note contains a brief description of the product, the manufacturer's suggested retail price, and the manufacturer's—or a supplier's—website address.

- The *Self-Assessment Questionnaire* icon usually flags a small questionnaire for you and your family to fill out. Occasionally, this icon will also appear next to a discussion that asks you to think about how you react in certain situations. Based on your answers, we'll suggest which alternative scheduling solution is likely to work better for you.

- The *Time Optimizer* icon appears next to examples of how to accomplish certain tasks more efficiently, so that you'll save time.

Our Goal

We know that many of you are overwhelmed by your current situation. This book is designed to help you get over the stumbling blocks that have been in your way until now.

- If you've tried various systems without success, this book will show you how to assess your family so that the next system you select is a good fit and will work for your family.
- If you think you're too busy just getting through the days to find time to organize your family's schedule, this book will let you do it a little at a time, with the promise that your small investments of time will have a big payoff in no time.

Our goal is to change your situation from "too much to do; too little time" to "We do a lot, and we have time to enjoy it!"

Part 1

The Mechanics of Family Scheduling—Tools and Techniques

Selecting a Planner

Things You'll Need

- ☐ Paper
- ☐ Pen/pencil
- ☐ Internet access (optional)

Planners come in all shapes, sizes, and configurations. Each one of them was designed by someone who thought he had improved upon the others. That's because different people's brains process, store, and retrieve information in different ways. Just as you won't wear a shirt if you don't like the color, you won't wear a pair of shoes if they hurt your feet, and you won't buy a golf club that doesn't improve your swing, you don't want to buy a planner that doesn't fit your family. So, if you've tried to organize your family's schedule before, but without success, don't despair! You probably were using a planner that was a bad fit.

Finding the right planner for an entire family may seem to be an impossible task. But if you follow the steps in this chapter, you're sure to pick a winner.

In this chapter:

- ✳ Understanding what each type of planner can and can't do
- ✳ Comparing hard-copy and electronic planners
- ✳ Assessing which style of planner will work for your family
- ✳ Purchasing a planner that meets your family's needs

Considering Types of Planners

The first step in selecting a planner for your family is to get a basic understanding of the various types of planners that are available and what each type can and can't do for you.

In today's world, you will find two basic types of planners: hard-copy planners and electronic planners. Each comes in a variety of sizes and formats. Read on to learn more about these varieties of planners and how they can work for you.

Hard-Copy Planners

When you think of a hard-copy planner, probably paper comes to mind. But not all hard-copy planners are made of paper. You can have a whiteboard, a laminated wipe-off surface, or a wall planner with moveable magnets.

The real defining features of hard-copy planners are

- All data must be input and manipulated manually.
- Information cannot be retrieved from a remote location.
- No power source is needed to operate them.
- They create a tactile connection with the user.

Hard-copy planners have certain advantages over their electronic counterparts:

- Data cannot be lost inadvertently.
- They are easy to use.

Planner Sizes

As with all things where you have a choice, each option carries with it certain plusses and minuses. The size of your planner will determine where you will locate it, how much information you can put on it, and how many people will be able to use it.

A *wall-size* planner allows you to see most of the information in one view. It's large enough for all family members to add their information. And, because it stays in one place, it's impossible to lose. However, because the idea is to write the information large enough to be seen from a distance, the amount of detail you can include may be limited. A wall planner for the family is not meant to be personalized, and its size and fixed placement don't allow you to take it with you. You'll have to copy down any information—phone numbers, shopping lists, and the like—that you'll need when you leave the area.

A *desk-size* unit gives you more room to write down details. Because it's still fairly large—usually the size of a notepad—more than one person can add information to it. But, because it's portable and each family member may move it around while using it, it may get misplaced. And if someone doesn't know where it is at any given moment, that person will be less likely to use it.

Pocket-size planners are ideal for individual use. They can be highly personalized with all sorts of information that's relevant only to the one person who's using it. When it comes to family scheduling, pocket planners are best used as individual organizing tools, with each person copying down relevant information from the larger, more centralized wall or desk planner.

Planner Formats

How much of the family's schedule do you want or need to see at any given time? Your answer will go a long way to determining what format you'd like your planner to have.

A *yearly* format—usually wall-sized, but also available in desk-size—is a great visual tool that allows everyone in the family to see what lies ahead. This feature can be particularly important if you need all family members to know when they are expected to keep their schedules open for family events such as vacations, reunions, or spring cleaning.

We are all more familiar, however, with the *monthly* format. The best example of this format is a traditional wall calendar that has one page per month with every day represented as a square on the monthly grid. The biggest drawback with these calendars is that you can put an event on a certain day, but there usually isn't any way to put it into a specific time slot. As a result, you can easily overlook a conflict if two activities take place at the same time.

Weekly formats provide you with room for a lot more details, such as who's participating in an activity and at exactly what time. You can also start to list things that aren't major events or activities but are still things that need to be done to keep your family running smoothly—things such as picking up the dry cleaning or preparing dinner.

Daily planners drill things down to the finest detail. You can start to look at things minute-by-minute. This way, you can plan for things like travel time to the soccer game. A daily planner can be a life-changer for you if you're the type of person who always seems to run late for things. Scheduling anything too tightly, though, can take the spontaneity and fun out of anyone's day. And hyperfocusing can cause everyone in the family to lose sight of the big picture.

ACHIEVING THE RIGHT BALANCE

Most likely you've decided that you want to organize your family's schedule because your family isn't getting things done when they should or is forgetting some things altogether. Or perhaps you've just been waiting to get organized until you can be sure you'll do it right. Either way, the stress is likely to cause you to look for a system that will have your family running with machine-like precision. This sort of idealization of the "perfect" schedule may well cause you to have an inclination to hyperfocus on your schedule's details with questions such as "Does it take me two minutes or three to walk to the mailbox and get the mail?" This quest for perfection will just lead to more anxiety and the risk of losing your ability to be a spontaneous and fun-loving person.

The solution is for you to find a system that allows you to be confident that you have everything that needs to be done—along with the things you want to do—on the schedule and that you can accomplish them at a comfortable pace. You don't want to pack your schedule so tightly that you can't take time for spontaneous and serendipitous events such as watching baby birds learn to fly, visiting with a friend who's unexpectedly in from out of town, or helping out a colleague. The overall goal of this book is to help you establish this sort of balanced schedule for your whole family.

User Bases

Another variable you'll want to consider when choosing a planner is the number of people who can use it. The bigger your family, the more selective you'll have to be to get a planner that can accommodate everyone's schedules. Personal planners— pocket planners or desk models that have room for personal goals—can work really well for some individuals, but when it comes to an entire family's schedule, you're going to need some sort of centralized system that holds the master list of everyone's information.

If one family member is in charge of managing the entire household's schedule and is willing to act as the schedule's clearinghouse, then an individual planner might work. But the whole effort of organizing your family's schedule will be much easier if you're willing to set up a multiuser planner to which everyone can have easy access. That doesn't mean you can't pair your "schedule central" with portable planners for family members who have complicated schedules and need more than a quick glance at the main schedule every morning.

So, if you're going to select a hard-copy planner, then size, format, and user base are all factors you'll want to evaluate. Table 1.1 helps you do that by providing an at-a-glance comparison of these features.

Table 1.1   Comparison of Hard-Copy Planners

Format	Size	Multiuser	Portable	Detailed
Yearly	Wall	✓		
	Desk	✓	✓	
	Pocket		✓	
Monthly	Wall	✓		
	Desk	✓	✓	
	Pocket		✓	
Weekly	Wall	✓		✓
	Desk		✓	✓
	Pocket		✓	✓
Daily	Wall	✓		✓
	Desk		✓	✓
	Pocket		✓	✓

Using a Daily Group Planner

If, in the final analysis, your family decides that what you need is a daily planner that you can all use together, you can get a more highly specialized product known as a daily group planner. Figure 1.1 illustrates how you can use this product to record and view each family member's daily schedule next to each other. That way, you can see exactly what everyone is scheduled to be doing at any given time of any given day.

tip

If you want to use a desk-type planner for your whole family, consider propping it up in a book holder. This positioning will make the planner easy to see and keep it from getting buried and lost under other papers.

Electronic Planners

When you think of an electronic planner, you probably envision a pocket-sized digital assistant. But not all electronic planners are small single-user units. You can have an electronic planner on your desktop computer or on the Internet. You can even find countertop electronic planners meant for the whole family to use.

Tuesday, May 17

	Mom	Dad	Dick	Jane
8:00	leave for work		band	
8:15		Jane's carpool	practice	
8:30	staff			
8:45	meeting			
9:00				art museum
9:15				field trip
9:30				
9:45				
10:00				

The following are the real defining features of
electronic planners:

- Data can be re-sorted into various formats
  at the touch of a button.
- Recurring events need to be entered only
  once.
- They can be set to provide an auditory
  reminder (alarm) for an event.
- They need a power source to operate.

note AT-A-GLANCE makes both a Four-Person Daily Group Appointment Book (product #70-822) suggested retail: $42.89, and an Eight-Person Daily Group Appointment Book (product #70-212) suggested retail: $45.49. Website: www.ataglance.com

Electronic planners have certain advantages over their hard-copy counterparts:

- They store an incredible amount of detailed information in a very small
  space.
- The information can be easily cross-referenced and backed up.
- The information is less available for public view.

Determining Planner Accessibility

If you choose to use an electronic planner for organizing your family's schedule,
you'll want to think about how and where you'll want to be able to access the information you put into it.

A piece of scheduling software together with your desktop computer—or even your laptop, for that matter—will have incredible capabilities. You'll be able to cross reference an event by person, date, or frequency. You'll be able to link the event to driving directions, addresses, phone numbers, and more. In fact, you'll be able to manipulate the data in far more ways than you would ever want or have the time to do! And you must consider the disadvantages, too. You'd have to boot up the computer every time you wanted to check or change the schedule. If someone else were using the computer, you might forget you needed to add something by the time your turn to use it came around. And if you ever wanted to take a piece of the schedule with you, you'd have to print it out on paper.

> **note**
>
> Product Note
>
> NetSimplicity's Family Scheduler is designed to let you track what your whole family is doing by day, week, or month. Windows PC users can download a 15-day free trial. Suggested retail: $49. Website: www.netsimplicity.com

If you have a lot of family members who are away from home most of the day but have access to computers, you might want to consider using an electronic planner that has remote access. Essentially, this type of system lets the authorized users upload information into their planner; that information is then stored on a server and accessed by way of the Internet. See the sidebar "Finding an Online Organizer" for more information.

FINDING AN ONLINE ORGANIZER

You can find a lot of options for an online planner by using your favorite web browser and searching for *online calendar* or *personal online organizer*. As with most things Internet related, the ones that are free will be full of advertisements. However, don't despair! For a modest cost—usually less than the cost of a software program or a paper planner—you can have an online planner ad-free. Keep in mind that you'll encounter the same drawbacks present in any personal computer–based electronic planners—needing access to the computer and having to print out information if you want to take it with you—if you choose a remote-access Internet-based option.

You're probably already familiar, at least in theory, with the various personal digital assistants (PDAs) available today. As Figure 1.2 shows, you can have them display your schedule in a monthly, weekly, or daily format. You can switch back and forth from one format to another at the touch of a button. You can keep your entire address and phone book in these units as well. And you can set timers to beep at you to remind you when you need to do things. You can even get a PDA built into your cellular phone. Even so, you must keep in mind that each unit is designed to be used fairly exclusively by one person only.

note Calendars Net provides online calendar hosting. Cost: free with ads; $18 per year ad-free. Website: www.calendars.net

Collabrio's MyEvents combines a web calendar, contact manager, task lists, and more. You can try it free for 15 days. Cost: $48 per year. Website: www.myevents.com

FIGURE 1.2

These screenshots of a Palm OS PDA show how you can display your calendar in various layouts depending on which format suits your needs at any given time.

If you decide an electronic planner is right for your family, but you're concerned about the drawbacks we've listed, then you might want to consider a specialized product that is designed to be a dedicated, multiuser electronic family planner. One such product is the Simpliciti Family Organizer shown in Figure 1.3. All family members can keep their own schedules and to do lists. But the schedules can also be viewed in combination. The unit comes with a small printer you can attach to it, so that you can easily print out the day's schedule or shopping list for one person or the whole family. If you mount it on the wall, this planner will stay put. It turns on instantly, so it is always ready for family members to add new information or take a printout with them.

Comparing Electronic Planners

If you're starting to feel overwhelmed by all of your options, Table 1.2 should help you sort out some of the variables you'll want to think about

note The Simpliciti Home Organizer shown in Figure 1.3 sits on a counter or mounts on a wall. Suggested retail: $129.95. Website: www.simpliciti.com

with respect to electronic planners. Then you should read on so that you can start to get a feel for which features will be important to each individual member of your family.

FIGURE 1.3
By providing a compact, dedicated, multiuser electronic planner, the Simpliciti Home Organizer bridges the gap between cumbersome desktop and laptop computers and single-user PDAs.

Table 1.2   Comparison of Electronic Planners

	Multiuser	Remote Access	Portable	Printable
Desktop computer	Limited	No	No	Yes
Internet	Limited	Yes	No	Yes
Handheld personal digital assistant	No	No	Yes	No
Specialized multiuser unit	Yes	No	Yes	Yes

To do list

☐ Have family members fill out the self-assessment questionnaire to determine what type of planner is best for them

☐ Choose the family member who'll take central responsibility for the planner

☐ Decide what type of planner fits your "master planner's" style, your family's activity patterns, and your family's needs

Choosing the Right Planner

As we said at the beginning of this chapter, the designer of each planner on the market today thought that his design was better than everyone else's. With so many choices out there, the question becomes which one of them is the right design for you and your family.

Filling Out the Self-Assessment Questionnaire

The self-assessment questionnaires in Tables 1.3 and 1.4 will help you match the right type of planner with each member of your family. Then, from the composite of answers, you'll be able to move forward in getting the right combination of tools.

Here's how to use the questionnaires:

1. On separate sheets of paper, have each family member answer the questions. If you have children under 10 years old, have them answer the alternate questionnaire found in Table 1.4.

2. For each set of answers, add the number of *a*'s and the number of *b*'s. The more *b*'s, the more likely the person will prefer to use an electronic planner. The more *a*'s, the more likely the person will prefer to use a hard-copy planner.

3. If, by some amazing chance, everyone in the family ends up having a score that prefers the same type of planner, then the task of selecting your tools for organizing your family's schedule is well on its way. More likely, however, you'll find a split among preferences, and that situation will require a little more analysis before selecting your new system.

> **tip** Another great feature of almost all electronic organizers is the convenience of having to enter a recurring event only once. So, if piano lessons are every Wednesday from 4:00 to 5:00 p.m., you have to enter the information only for the first lesson and then tell the planner that this same event happens every Wednesday. And, voilà!, piano lessons will appear on your schedule every Wednesday until you tell the planner otherwise.

Table 1.3   Self-Assessment Questionnaire— Ages 10 and Up

Hard-Copy Planner or Electronic Planner?

	a	b
1. Which do you prefer?		
a. Watch the news on TV		
b. Read the news in the newspaper		

Table 1.3   Continued

Hard-Copy Planner or Electronic Planner?

	a	b
2. Do you frequently get absorbed in what you're doing and forget about the time? a. No b. Yes		
3. When going someplace new, which would you prefer to have? a. A map showing the route b. Written step-by-step directions		
4. On average, how many different people do you phone during any one month? a. 20 or fewer b. More than 20		
5. When attending a meeting or class, which are you most likely to do? a. Take a lot of notes b. Take only a few notes		
6. Do you tend to remember where on a page you wrote something down? a. Yes b. No		
7. When you get a new piece of equipment, do you read the instruction manual? a. Hardly ever b. Almost always		
8. When you read a book or article, do you flip back to review previous pages? a. Often b. Rarely		
9. Do you remember things better if you write them down? a. Yes b. No		
10. Do you print email that contains information you don't want to lose? a. Frequently b. Rarely		
Total		

The more times you answered *b*, the more likely you will prefer an electronic planner. Conversely, the more times you answered *a*, the more likely you'll prefer a hard-copy planner.

Table 1.4   Self-Assessment Questionnaire—Ages 2 to 10

Hard-Copy Planner or Electronic Planner?

	a	b
1. Which would you rather read (or have someone read to you)?		
a. A story book		
b. A book of poems		
2. Do you frequently get absorbed in what you're doing and forget about the time?		
a. No		
b. Yes		
3. Which would you rather do?		
a. Draw someone a picture		
b. Tell someone a story		
4. How often do you clean your room?		
a. Only when you have to		
b. Every week		
5. Which do you enjoy playing more?		
a. A game of hide-and-seek		
b. A game of cards		
Total		

The more times your child answered *b*, the more likely she will prefer an electronic planner. Conversely, the more times she answered *a*, the more likely she'll prefer a hard-copy planner.

These self-assessment questionnaires are designed to match your planner selection to your learning style. In a family with diverse learning styles, you should select a family planner based on the majority preference. You'll be able to accommodate all family members individually when we discuss more personalized planning tools later in this book.

FINDING A PLANNER TO FIT THE WAY YOU THINK

Maybe you're wondering why some systems appeal to certain people, whereas completely different systems appeal to others. Part of the reason has to do with the way each individual's brain is wired. In simplistic terms, laymen often talk about people being right-brained or left-brained. In broad generalities, left-brained people (often right-handed) tend to be more mathematical and more linear thinkers. And right-brained people (often left-handed) tend to be more verbal and more creative types. Of course, people use both sides of their brain, just like they use both hands. It's just that one of the sides is dominant. And the more we learn about the brain, the more we realize that the way it functions is not nearly so clear-cut as just right and left.

Also, different people learn and remember information differently. They have different learning or functioning styles or modalities. Each person has a dominant modality, which is determined by genetics. Each person also has a preferred modality, which is the one in which the person was most taught to do something. Just as some left-handed people golf or knit right-handed because it's the way they were taught, so, too, people can favor different modalities based on early environmental factors.

In broad terms, you'll frequently hear people refer to three learning modalities: visual, auditory, and kinesthetic. In other words, some people learn by seeing, some by hearing, and some by doing. And, although one of the methods may predominate, the others still act as reinforcers. The more we find out about learning modalities, the less cut and dried they appear. For example, a visual learner may prefer seeing something, reading about it, or looking at a graphic representation of it. An auditory learner may learn better from hearing the material aloud or by reading with music in the background. Or a kinesthetic learner might prefer moving something around, writing about it, or just touching it.

What does this discussion have to do with selecting your family's planner? Actually, a lot. Just as when your shoes hurt your feet, you'll kick them off at the first chance you get, people will avoid using a planner that isn't comfortable for them. If this happens in your family, the scheduling system you've carefully created will break down. But when a tool fits a person's thinking and learning styles, the person feels comfortable with it. And when the person feels comfortable, he'll use it.

Determining Which Planner Is Best for Your Family

Now that everyone has answered the questionnaire and you have a preliminary idea of whether to select a hard-copy planner or an electronic one, you still need to factor in a few more items before you're ready to go to the store and make your purchase. No matter what you're organizing, theory is great, but it needs to be tempered with a healthy dose of practicality.

Matching the Style of the "Master Planner"

One important decision your family will need to make is who will be the person overseeing the family's schedule—the master planner, if you will. We're not talking here about the person who decides who will do what when. As you'll learn as you read through Parts II and III of this book, each family member should be an active participant in determining the family's schedule. The master planner is simply the person who makes sure that the master schedule is kept up-to-date and free of conflicts. The master planner stays on top of the schedule so she can call attention to any potential problems before they develop.

Stereotypically, the master planner has been the mother of the family, but there is really no reason why it has to be that way. Rather than allowing mom to become the master planner by default, you should give careful consideration to who can best fill this important role for the family. Of course, if the family has a stay-at-home parent, that parent is probably the one who has the most interest in making sure that the family schedule stays on track. Here are other qualities that can help you determine your family's best master planner:

- The family member who most likes to coordinate events
- The person with the most time
- A person with a strong sense of responsibility
- The person most committed to making the schedule work
- A person whose style matches the type of family planner you're going to use (check the person's individual responses to the self-assessment questionnaire)

Matching Your Family's Activity Patterns

You'll also want to look at the pattern of activities that will fill your days and your planner. Thinking ahead can make all the difference between getting a planner that will allow you to set up an efficient system and one that will require extra time and effort to maintain. Figures 1.4 and 1.5 show how one set of activities is better served by a horizontal format, whereas another set of activities is better served by a vertically formatted planner. Figure 1.6 shows how a mix of these activities can be handled easily with an electronic planner.

FIGURE 1.4

If your family has more activities that take place on every day of certain weeks, then a horizontal format, with the days of the week listed across the page, makes entering the activities on the calendar easier.

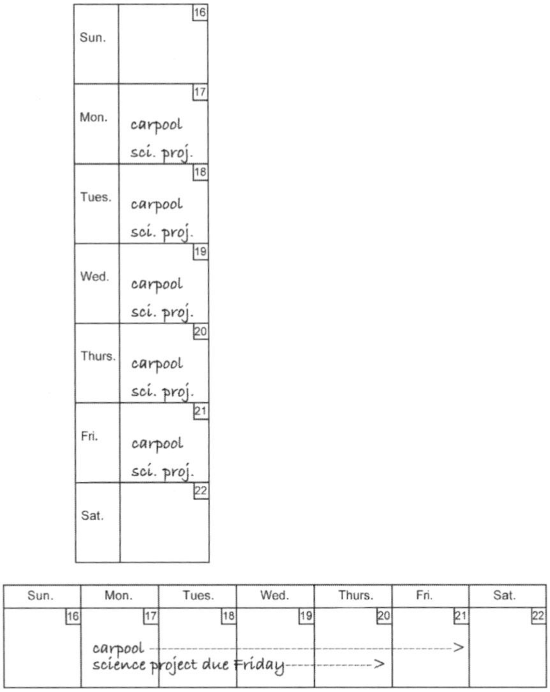

	16
Sun.	

	17
Mon.	carpool sci. proj.

	18
Tues.	carpool sci. proj.

	19
Wed.	carpool sci. proj.

	20
Thurs.	carpool sci. proj.

	21
Fri.	carpool sci. proj.

	22
Sat.	

Sun.	Mon.	Tues.	Wed.	Thurs.	Fri.	Sat.
16	17	18	19	20	21	22
	carpool --> science project due Friday--------------->					

FIGURE 1.5

If your family has more weekly activities—those that take place once a week—a vertical format, with the days of the week listed down the side of the page, is more efficient.

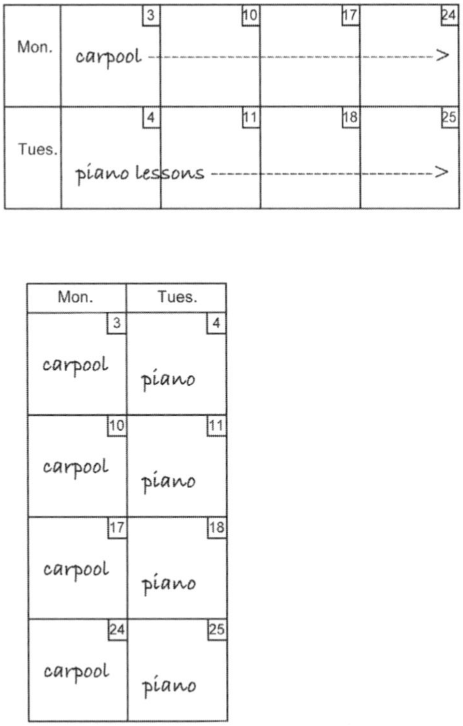

	3	10	17	24
Mon.	carpool -->			

	4	11	18	25
Tues.	piano lessons -------------------------------->			

Mon.	Tues.
3	4
carpool	piano
10	11
carpool	piano
17	18
carpool	piano
24	25
carpool	piano

FIGURE 1.6

FIGURE 1.6
With an electronic planner, you can record week-long events and weekly events with equal ease.

Other Important Considerations

If you've chosen a type of planner that's not portable—and you really should want the main planner to stay in one place—you'll need to decide which family members need to take their schedules with them. Then you'll need to add a portable format for each of those people. The great flexibility here is that each person can choose whether he wants a hard-copy or electronic portable version.

Bear in mind that the age of your family members will also influence the type of planner you'll want to select. The adults in the family may be perfectly happy with electronic planners, but if the children are all in their preschool years, you'll want to remember that they'll need something more tangible and less tied to the written word if you want them to understand the schedule and become actively involved in making sure it works. Age-appropriate planners can be valuable supplements to the main schedule and will be explained more thoroughly in Part III.

The one overriding consideration in picking the family planner is to select the most inclusive planner you can find while making sure that no one in the family is alienated by it.

Purchasing Your Planner

By now, you're probably eager to get out there, purchase your planning tools, and get your family's schedule organized. So this section will give you some dollars-and-cents advice about what to get. However, even with all of the information we've already covered about what types of planners work best in what types of situations and for what people, it's really still a little early in the game to buy a lot of equipment with total confidence. As you read the rest of the book, we'll explore a lot of the often-overlooked areas of family scheduling, as well as some specialized tools for people in specific situations. So, you might want to hold off making a final decision on your planner until after you've read through the rest of the book. It won't take too long; that's a promise!

Table 1.5 will give you some idea of the annual cost of each of the systems we've outlined. Keep in mind that, in some cases, you'll need more than one of the components. For example, if you opt for a piece of family scheduling software for your family's computer, individual members might want a portable system—hand-held digital assistant, two-year pocket calendar, or day-by-day pocket diary—to carry along with them.

Table 1.5   Cost Comparison of Planners

Type of Planner	Yearly Cost
Hard Copy	
Wall–yearly/monthly–laminated/wipe-off	$20–28
Wall–yearly–dry-erase board	$65
Wall–monthly–dry-erase board	$85
Wall–monthly–magnetic	$165–450
Wall–monthly–paper	$12–25
Desk–monthly–calendar	$8–25
Desk–monthly–portable planner	$25–40
Desk–weekly–planner	$10–50
Desk–daily–one page per day	$5–25
Desk–daily–portable planner	$20–60
Desk–daily–4-person and 8-person planners	$45
Pocket–yearly/monthly–calendar	$5
Pocket–monthly/weekly/daily–planner	$20–60
Electronic	
Calendar/scheduling software for desktop computers*	$50
Personalized online calendars	$0–130
Personal digital assistants (per unit)	$80–800
Multiuser digital assistant with printer	$130

*Cost of computer not included.

The prices listed are manufacturers' suggested retail prices. Don't hesitate to shop around online and in discount office supply stores for the best prices.

Chapter Summary

Here we are at the end of Chapter 1, and you've already learned a lot:

- You know that there are basically two types of planners: hard copy and electronic.
- You're aware that each type comes in a wide array of formats with a wide variety of features.
- You understand that each individual will have a propensity toward one type and certain formats.
- You've learned how to determine which planner will work best for your family and why.
- You understand the market well enough to make an informed purchase.

Before leaving this chapter, use the following checklist to make sure you haven't missed a critical step in organizing your family's schedule.

- ❏ Review the types of planners available and their respective capabilities.
- ❏ Have everyone in your family answer the self-assessment questionnaire.
- ❏ Decide which family member will oversee the family's schedule.
- ❏ Decide which type of planner fits your family's pattern of activities and won't alienate any individual family member.
- ❏ Take some time to shop around online and in office supply stores.

Having the right tools is very important for success. Using the tools is critical. So, next we'll look at how to set up your new system.

Setting Up Your Planner

2

Setting up your planner and learning how to use it are critical to successfully organizing your family's schedule. Just as a hammer sitting on your workbench won't drive a nail all by itself, your new planner left buried under a pile of papers on your dining room table won't manage your family's schedule.

This chapter shows you how to develop just the right scheduling system for you and your family. You'll learn how to find the right place to keep your planner, get the whole family involved in using it, and manage the kinds of information you'll keep in it. You'll also learn how using your new system can help you eliminate clutter.

Now the care we took in Chapter 1, "Selecting a Planner," to select the right planner for your family will pay big dividends. When you buy a new outfit that looks and feels great, you can't wait to wear it. Your new planner should look and feel great so that you can't wait to use it. (Of course, waiting till you've read through the rest of this book will guarantee that you have the right accessories as well.)

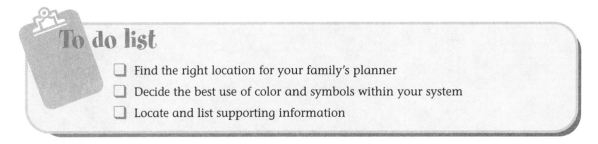

To do list

- [ ] Find the right location for your family's planner
- [ ] Decide the best use of color and symbols within your system
- [ ] Locate and list supporting information

Developing a System for Your Hard-Copy Planner

If your family has selected a hard-copy planner (or if you're still considering this option), then this section is for you. You'll design a location to keep your new planner and put in place the basic system that you'll be using to organize your family's schedule.

Things You'll Need

- [ ] Your new planner
- [ ] Nails and hammer, screws and screwdriver, thumbtacks, tape, or magnets (as appropriate for installation)
- [ ] Pens and pencils
- [ ] Colored markers (optional)
- [ ] Family address book information and phone numbers
- [ ] Phone-messaging pad (optional)

Deciding Where to Locate the Planner

The real estate business has a popular saying: "location, location, location." Your entire system will fail if you don't locate your planner in the right place. Do you doubt it? Have you ever ruined a kitchen knife by using it as a makeshift screwdriver because going to the basement to get the screwdriver seemed like too much trouble? But if the screwdriver had been in the kitchen, you would have reached for it first. Location!

caution Remember, the planner may fit perfectly in a spot and look very artistic, but you must not give in to form at the cost of function.

For many families, the kitchen is the hub of their home. It's the room where they eat, talk on the phone, do homework, work on craft projects, and post notices on the bulletin board or refrigerator. There's nothing wrong with picking this same room as the location for your family planner. The key reason, though, is not because it's the kitchen, but because it's the family hub. Take a look at Table 2.1 for some other characteristics that will help you determine your own family hub and a good location for your organizing command center.

tip Don't place a wipe-off planner where there will be a lot of steam—near the stovetop or a shower—because the moisture will cause the ink to run.

Table 2.1   Do's and Don'ts for Choosing a Planner Location

DO Put It	DON'T Put It
Where everyone in the family will see it	Where every visitor will see it
Where the most family members gather at one time	In a bedroom (or any other room that doesn't belong to the whole family)
Where family members pass it as they enter or leave the house	Where it will be exposed to extreme heat, cold, or moisture
Near a phone	Where the dog will eat it
In a place where nothing else belongs	Where it will interfere with traffic flow or activities
In easy reach	Where it will get moved

We hope you won't have too much trouble determining the room where your planner belongs. Proper location, however, doesn't end with room selection. You'll also want to look at the placement of your planner from an ergonomic point of view. Consider these points:

- Make sure the planner is placed at a good height. The more people you have in your family, the harder this one becomes. Short people need the planner lower than tall people. If your kids' ages span a wide range, finding the best height for the planner can be a challenge. If you think about this issue from a functional standpoint, though, you may find the solution. Preschoolers will probably have their own set of tools to manage their simpler schedules (see Chapter 8, "Managing the Preschool Years"). All that these young children need is to be able to see that the family planner exists and has a purpose. Teenagers, who are, of course, taller, will be expected to take a more active role in contributing to and following the schedule. So, placing the planner where they can see and reach it easily is more important.

- Make sure the planner is accessible in other ways besides height. Does your family have some members who are right-handed and others who are left-handed? Then you need to place the planner so that members can write on it with either hand. If you place it with its left side flush up against a corner, then a left-handed person will have no way of writing on it without bashing his elbow or contorting his stance. If someone in your house wears bifocals, then it's way more difficult for that person to focus when looking down at something in close range than when looking up at something in close range.

- Safety first! Avoid positioning the planner where someone using it will be likely to reach across or lean against something hot, such as the stove, the toaster, or a radiator. Avoid a place where someone might lean in a direction that could cause her to fall down stairs or where she will try to brace herself against something slippery or breakable.

> **note** Don't overlook the importance of accommodating anyone in your family who is physically challenged. Someone with two strong legs can climb or stoop if need be, but someone in a wheelchair or with arthritis or a bad back cannot.

Using Color and Symbols

As we've already explored, some people find it easier to assimilate information if they can see a picture or map rather than written words. This preference in learning modalities has nothing to do with age or intelligence.

However, we can certainly say that most children can identify colors, shapes, and objects significantly earlier than they can read. It would make sense, then, that a family with a young child would benefit from incorporating color and symbols into their planner. The child could learn that she is involved in anything that appears on the planner in a certain color or anything that is marked by a sticker with her picture on it. If you're marking off blocks of time for an activity and the blocks are color-coded, your child will start learning about time, too. She'll learn that small blocks on the planner are activities that take less time than the ones that are represented by bigger blocks.

Even when everyone is old enough to read the words on the planner, people who respond better to color and symbols will like a color-coded system. You can use a different color for each person. Or you can use a different color for each category of activities, such as school/work, sports, chores, and errands. As long as you don't use too many colors, the color helps the brain sort and process the information more quickly because more information is taken in with a single glance.

Color and symbols have their drawbacks, too. Table 2.2 outlines some of the advantages and disadvantages of using color.

Table 2.2   Plusses and Minuses of Using Color on Your Planner

Color Plusses	Color Minuses
Young children can identify and understand colors.	If used inconsistently, color can create confusion.
Some people respond better to color than to black and white.	More thought is required when entering information.
Color can help people sort information into categories at a glance.	Using color requires a larger, better-maintained stock of supplies.

Because of the drawbacks, you may want to make doubly sure that the benefit to at least one member of your family will outweigh the negatives. If you think about the way the person reacts to things in everyday life, you'll get a feel for his style. Use the questions in Table 2.3 to help you with your evaluation.

Table 2.3   Self-Assessment Questionnaire

Will Color Help You?

	a	b

1. When you're driving down the road, which do you seem to notice more?
    a.   Street signs
    b. Landmarks		

2. Do you sometimes reach for the wrong box of cereal in the grocery store because the package is the same color as the box of the cereal you really want?
    a.   No
    b. Yes		

3. What palate of clothing do you prefer?
    a.   Earth toned
    b. Brightly colored		

4. How often do you use color to help describe an object ("red truck," "blue flower")?
    a.   Rarely
    b. Almost always		

If you answered more *a*'s than *b*'s, color-coding your planner is probably not worth the trouble.

Using color will work only if you use it consistently, which means that you can't just pick up the nearest pencil and write something onto the schedule. If you've written it in the wrong color, at best you've destroyed the system, and at worst you've caused confusion. So, you must always have all of the colors available for use. If you're using only four colors, and you're willing to let one of them be black, you can get a pen that writes in all four colors—it has four ink barrels—and attach it to your planner. Then you just need to make sure you always select the correct color before writing something down.

note The BIC 4-Color Pen provides four-color—black/blue/green/red—writing convenience in a single pen. Suggested retail: $2.34. Website:www.bicworld.com

Using Your Planner

Now it's time to put your planner to use. Our best advice here is to start slowly, establish a solid foundation, and continue to build on it. Remember when you learned to type? Of course, you wanted to be able to make your fingers fly across the keyboard producing pages of text right from the start. Instead, you were forced to begin with exercises that limited you to just two or four letters. When you had mastered those letters, you were allowed to add a couple of new letters. In the end, your brain could send signals to your fingers without any conscious thought on your part; you'd think about what you wanted to type and your fingers would type it.

So, ease into using your new system by putting just a few of the most obvious items on it. Add previously scheduled events as you think of them. Add new events as they come up. Add things the family is forgetting to do as you are reminded of them. At least at the beginning, you don't need to spend time writing down all of the things you're remembering to do anyway. Your planner will have the most immediate positive impact if you can get it to help you with just a few things that your family is currently neglecting to do. Then, in the chapters that follow, you will build on that foundation and craft your family's schedule into a smooth-running tool.

YOUR FAMILY'S PATH TO AN ORGANIZED SCHEDULE

Doing anything for the first time is like forging through the wilderness. Then, just as the trip becomes easier when you take the same route a second and third time and you start to wear a path, so does the task become easier each time you repeat it. In a sense, you are beating a path through your brain. When you first perform the task, a series of neural transmitters create a weak pathway in your brain. Then, with each repetition and more neural transmissions, the path is strengthened. Soon the pathway is well established and will stay there for a long time, even if you don't use it. That's why breaking a habit is so hard. In the past, some efficiency experts have called this "finger memory," because after a while the path is so strong that your fingers will do what they're supposed to without your thinking about it at all. Examples include touch typing, peeling an apple, and using a gear shift.

If you couple this brain process with your natural tendencies, you can create a brain superhighway. Let's continue with the path analogy. On some college campuses, a landscape architect plants a large expanse of grass. Then he sits back and waits to see where the students naturally create paths with their walking patterns. Then he has paved walkways installed where the most students walk. On other campuses, the architect installs the paved walkways first. Then the beauty of his landscape becomes marred as students take shortcuts across the grass anyway. Sometimes a rigid administration decides to put up fences—pretty bushes or ugly chain-link—to keep the students on the predesignated paths. How frustrating!

What do paths on college campuses have to do with organizing your family's schedule? You've already selected a planner that conforms to your family's natural tendencies (the wait-and-see-where-they-walk approach). Next, you need to watch to see where the system doesn't quite work out as planned (where the shortcuts are taken). Then, as a final commitment to keeping your family's schedule organized, you must make sure that you don't build any fences that frustrate the system's users.

When your family finds the paths they need to take to be where they would naturally go, the system will become so ingrained in their brains that success is inevitable.

Maintaining Supporting Information

After you begin to work with your planner, you'll quickly realize that if you want to be efficient, you'll need to have more information at your fingertips than just a calendar of your family's events and activities. Here's a checklist of some of this vital information:

- Phone numbers
  - ☐ School
  - ☐ Teachers
  - ☐ Friends
  - ☐ Pizza delivery
  - ☐ Doctor
  - ☐ Repair people
- Addresses
  - ☐ Friends
  - ☐ Extended family
  - ☐ Business associates
- Invitations
  - ☐ Events requiring RSVP
  - ☐ Events you'll attend
- Phone messages

You can keep a short list of phone numbers and addresses right on (or next to) the planner itself. Ideally, you'll keep your family's personal address/phone book and your city's phone book nearby as well.

If everyone contributes to keeping a log of incoming phone calls, you can keep missed phone messages to a minimum. A two-part carbonless phone message pad allows you to take a copy of the message with you and still keep a permanent record in case you lose the tear-slip. As shown in Figure 2.1, the most versatile of these message pads come with tear-slips that are also sticky notes.

note Adams Write 'N Stick Message Book, shown in Figure 2.1, can hold 220 phone messages. Suggested retail: $6.29. Website: www.cardinalbrands.com

Product Note

A good hard-copy family scheduling system is intuitive to use. Let everyone in the family know that this tool is there to make life easier. Then just start using the planner and refer your family members to it often, and the system will naturally develop into your family's "command center."

FIGURE 2.1
This two-part carbon-less phone message book features removable sticky-note messages that can be placed where they won't be missed, such as on a door, on a computer monitor, in a day planner, or almost anywhere.

To do list

- ❏ Choose a location for your computer (or planner unit) and printer if you're using a desktop system
- ❏ Enter your family's schedule for the next two weeks
- ❏ Enter your family address book and phone number information (if it's not already entered into the scheduling software)
- ❏ Schedule family training session(s) to teach everyone to use the system
- ❏ Prepare backup system/disks

Developing a System for Your Electronic Planner

If your family has selected an electronic planner (or if you're still considering this option), then this section is for you. Here, you'll learn how to set up your electronic scheduling system, train your family in its use, and make sure you've input all the supporting information you'll need to keep the system running smoothly. Finally, you'll set up a good backup system to make sure your electronic schedule is kept safe from crashes, viruses, and other hazards.

Things You'll Need

- [ ] Electronic scheduling software
- [ ] Computer, desktop planner unit, or PDA
- [ ] Power source
- [ ] Instruction manual
- [ ] Family address book information and phone numbers
- [ ] Printer paper
- [ ] Backup disks

Setting Up the System

You need to deal with an entirely different set of factors when setting up an electronic planning system. If you've chosen a desktop or remote-access planner, then where you locate the system will be predetermined, in large part, by the type of computer setup your family is already using. Table 2.4 highlights some of the main considerations.

Table 2.4   Locating a Shared Desktop Computer

DO Put It	DON'T Put It
In a room that the whole family uses	Where it will be exposed to extreme heat, cold, or moisture
Near a phone	Where it will interfere with traffic flow or activities

If your family uses a network of computers, then central location will not be a major factor; it's simply important that each family member who's old enough to use the system has access to a computer that will display the planner. (Note: A free-standing computer that is not networked to the computer that houses the family's planner will not do the trick.) If you think that various family members will be printing out part of the schedule to help them accomplish their responsibilities, then make sure that the printer they will use is located where they can get to it at all times.

Ergonomics remain important. You'll want to ensure that the lighting in the room illuminates the screen without causing a glare, that the keyboard is placed at a comfortable height, and that the chair provides adequate support and mobility.

If you've chosen a dedicated, multiuser planning device, the considerations of where to locate it are similar to the considerations for hard-copy planners. (Refer to Table 2.1.) The one major difference is that you might want to keep the device out of the reach of young children who may find pushing the buttons—and inadvertently deleting data—too much of a temptation.

Setting up an electronic system takes time. (This is one of the reasons it is so important for you to determine whether your family has more of an affinity to this type of system than to a hard-copy one.) At the very least, someone will need to take the time to install or download the scheduling software.

Most of the products on the market are designed to be intuitive, but, even so, you'll save a lot of frustration—and missed appointments—if you take the time to read the instructions and learn some of the program's sophisticated capabilities.

note Printer ink is one of the most expensive liquids you can buy. It costs more than $17,000 per gallon!

Next, take the time to set up a full-blown version of your family's schedule for the next two weeks. Include all the cross-referencing to phone numbers, driving directions, and so on that you can. Consider color-coding carefully. There's no question that things are easier to separate visually and read on the screen if you use many different colors. However, printing out schedules that are created with color, even if you print them in grayscale, will use a lot more printer ink. It would be nice if the software gave you a print feature that provided a white (ink-free) background, but this doesn't seem to be a common option.

Remember to take advantage of the features that make electronic organizers unique. For example, if you invest the time up front to input the frequency with which an event recurs, you'll save the time later of having to input the event a 2nd, 3rd, or 52nd time. The only way you can justify all of the upfront effort of an electronic system is if it pays off in greater usability and time savings somewhere down the road.

COMMON WAYS TO MISSCHEDULE EVENTS USING AN ELECTRONIC PLANNER

One of the great advantages of electronic planners is that you can do so much at the touch of a button. However, when things happen at the touch of a button, mistakes can be made so quickly that they're not even noticed. If you use a PDA, watch out for these common mistakes:

1. Scheduling an event in the wrong half of the day. You can easily schedule something in the p.m. that should be in the a.m., and vice versa. It's very upsetting to have an alarm go off at 7:00 p.m. alerting you to your breakfast meeting at 7:30—that is, 7:30 a.m., which happened 11 1/2 hours ago.

2. Scheduling an event in the wrong year. Unlike a paper planner that probably covers only one or two years at a time, a PDA enables you to schedule events far into the future. Tap your stylus one too many times, and you could be scheduling next year's doctor's appointment two years from now.

Training Your Family to Use the Planner

One of the reasons you need to input at least two weeks' worth of data is so that you have something you can use to demonstrate the new system to your family. When you have the system ready to go, you need to make sure that everyone knows how to use it. You'll need to highlight and explain the features because so many of them are out of sight.

At a minimum, show your family how to

- Click through on an entry to get the underlying supporting information.
- Search for a particular event.
- Display the calendar by day, week, month, or year.
- Display the schedule by individual or group.
- Enter new events.
- Modify existing events.

Then set up some parameters for using the system:

- Who will be responsible for entering events? Each individual or one designated person.
- Must events be preapproved before being scheduled? All events, some events, or no events.
- How often must the calendar be updated? Daily, weekly, or somewhere in between.
- How often must each member check the schedule for changes? Daily, weekly, or somewhere in between.
- Do you want to have a mechanism for alerting other members to additions and changes? If so, by email or another method.

It's okay if the answers to these questions are not all the same for each family member as long as everyone understands each family member's obligations and privileges. This point bears repeating: The system will work only if all family members are comfortable with their roles.

Accessing Supporting Information

Most family scheduling and calendaring software dovetails with other database software. What does this mean to you? It means that if you've already entered your family's address book and phone book into a computer database, then you can link that information to your new scheduling software. So, when you set up an activity, you can link it to the phone number, address, and driving directions that are already on your computer's hard drive.

If you don't already have all of this information stored electronically, you'll want to start investing the time to build this support structure for your new system. Make sure, too, that someone is responsible for inputting new information as it becomes available. Having the piano teacher's new address posted on the refrigerator, instead of linked electronically to the piano lesson on the calendar, is the sort of thing that will quickly undermine the whole system.

Backing Up the Information

> **tip**
> If you watch the ads, you can usually get a nice supply of CDs to use as backup disks free, after rebate.

You hear it all the time: You must back up your computer files! It's not a question of "if" your hard drive crashes; it's a question of "when."

Before you go any further, decide who will be responsible for backing up all of your data weekly and schedule this activity on your calendar as a recurring weekly event for that person. It wouldn't hurt, at least in the beginning, to assign a second person to police the first person. Schedule that as a recurring weekly event, too.

Don't let backup disks become a source of clutter in your home. If you're using rewritable media, have two disks. Alternate their use: Use one the first week, the other the second week, the original one the third week, and so on. Every six months or so, throw the disks out and replace them with new ones. Schedule this switch as an event in your planner. This system will ensure that you always have a backup, even if one of the backup disks becomes corrupted. And always using relatively new disks reduces the chance of the disks becoming corrupted.

If you're using single-use disks, keep the current disk and the one from the week before. Throw out the third oldest disk every time you update.

ON THE HORIZON: THE ONCE AND FUTURE PDA-LINKING SOLUTION

The Palm Operating System (Palm OS) is the world's most widely used operating system for personal digital assistants. Wouldn't it be great if you could enter all of your family's events into your desktop computer using your Palm software and then have each member hot sync his handheld unit and end up with the family's joint events and his own personal items? At one time a piece of software called WeSync was available; it allowed families to do just that. The WeSync software is not available currently, but it has just been sold to a new company that plans to update it and put it back on the market. If you are interested in setting up this sort of system for your family, you can check the current status of the WeSync software at www.wesync.com.

To do list

- ❑ Review your family's planner regularly
- ❑ Make a note of what you need to do each day
- ❑ Check to see how your day's activities will be affected by other family members' schedules
- ❑ Select a portable system for information you need to carry with you
- ❑ Take everything you need with you when you leave the house

Managing the Information for Any Type of Planner

So, now you have this great repository of knowledge about your family's schedule. And, if it's electronic, when it's turned off and sitting there, it might just as well be a giant rock. Yes, we know we've told you to set up ground rules to have everyone check the schedule on a regular basis. But, whether it's hard-copy or electronic, you're going to need some way to make sure that all family members have the necessary information at their fingertips when they need it. In concrete terms, how are you going to make sure that your older son remembers to stop by the day care center to pick up his little sister on his way home from his trombone lesson?

If your family were on the cutting edge of technology, you'd have your schedule uploaded to a website coded for wireless access, and your son would take his web-enabled cell phone, access the family's calendar, and know exactly what he had to do. (You probably wouldn't feel the need to be reading this book, either.) Fortunately, you can find some more practical, less expensive ways to handle this situation, too.

Things You'll Need

- ❑ Your family's planner
- ❑ A portable planner for your individual use

Reviewing a Sample Schedule

Succinctly stated, each person needs to know what he has to do at any given time and how that relates to what the rest of the family is doing. We'll look at how to accomplish that using the simple sample family schedule shown in Table 2.5.

Table 2.5   Sample Family Schedule

	Mom	Dad	Older Brother	Younger Sister
8:00	drive to work		band practice	
8:30	staff meeting	take Sister to day care		day care
9:00	"	work	math test	
9:30	major project			
10:00	"			field trip to farm—take boots
10:30	"			"
11:00	"			"
11:30	"			"
noon	lunch with client	pay bills during lunch hour	buy yearbook at lunch	
12:30	"	"	"	
1:00	"			
1:30		sales meeting		
2:00		"		
2:30		"		
3:00				
3:30			trombone lesson	
4:00			"	
4:30			pick up Sister	
5:00	grocery shopping			
5:30	"	wrap birthday present		
6:00				
6:30	dinner at restaurant to celebrate Grandpa's birthday			
7:00	"	"	"	"
7:30	"	"	"	"
8:00	"	"	"	"
8:30				
9:00				
9:30				

You'll notice that Mom and Dad's work schedules are included in the family's planner. This combined work and home schedule lets each family member see how his plans will affect and be affected by everyone else's activities. From the sample schedule in Table 2.5, the family can determine the following details that will keep their day running smoothly.

Mom needs to make sure she is carrying with her the following information:

- Her work obligations for the day

  Staff meeting at 8:30

  Scheduled uninterrupted time from 9:30 to noon to work on a major project

  Lunch with a client at noon
- The grocery list because she's going to do the grocery shopping after work
- A note that she must be home by 6:00 to get to the birthday party on time
- A reminder that Dad won't be available by phone between 1:30 and 3:00

Dad needs to review the schedule before he leaves home so he remembers to do the following:

- Take Sister to day care, making sure she has her boots for the field trip
- Take the bills and checkbook with him so he can pay them during his lunch break

Dad also needs to make sure he is carrying with him the following information:

- His schedule for while he's at work

  Bill paying during lunch hour

  Sales meeting scheduled from 1:30 to 3:00
- A note that he must be home by 5:30 to wrap the birthday present and get to the birthday party on time
- A reminder that Mom won't be available by phone between 8:30 a.m. and 1:30 p.m.

Older Brother should be prepared for these activities before he leaves in the morning:

- Band practice, his math test, and his trombone lesson

He also needs to make sure he is carrying with him the following:

- Check or cash to buy his yearbook at lunch
- Trombone for his lesson at 3:30
- Reminder to pick up Sister at 4:30
- Reminder of birthday dinner at 6:30
- Phone numbers to reach Mom and Dad; he may want to note that if he needs to reach a parent, Dad's schedule is open in the morning and Mom's schedule is open in the afternoon

Younger Sister should be reminded in the morning, probably by Dad, of these items:

- She has a field trip to the farm (that's why she's taking her boots) and Grandpa's birthday dinner is tonight

Making the Scheduling Information Portable

Each family member can use a different method of taking his information with him. Mom and Dad may each choose to use

- A paper planner—Because of the level of detail they need for their office schedules, they'll probably want planners in either a weekly or daily format.
- A PDA—This device will hold all of the information they'll need compactly and privately.
- A computer printout—This option is workable only if the family is using an electronic scheduling system.

Because Mom and Dad work in offices where they have access to computers all day long, they could also use an online calendar. The advantage to them of an online calendar would be that

- They wouldn't have to copy over each day's schedule into a portable planner.
- If one of them entered new information into the planner, that new event would be instantly accessible by the other of them so that schedule conflicts could be avoided.

Older Brother won't have online access all day long, so he'll have to opt for a portable system. He, too, can choose from a paper planner, a PDA, or a computer printout. Because he may need to call one of his parents and he won't be sitting at a desk with a phone, he's likely to carry a cellular phone. He can easily use a built-in cell phone calendar to carry his day's reminders along with the phone numbers he may need. On the other hand, he may find that a simple assignment notebook is easier for him to use, especially because he's probably not allowed to enter assignments into his phone while he's in class.

Because Younger Sister is very young and isn't responsible for remembering where she needs to be at any given time, she doesn't need to take a copy of her schedule with her at all.

note Each person does not need to carry with him all of the details of every other family member's day.

If the family has chosen a multiuser PDA, such as the Simpliciti Family Organizer described in Chapter 1, each member can print off the day's reminders at the touch of a button before leaving the house in the morning. Mom, of course, will also print off the grocery list directly from the same unit.

To do list

- ☐ Put papers you'll need again soon in a sorter with labeled compartments
- ☐ Keep each family member's mail and papers separate from everyone else's
- ☐ Customize your sorter to fit your family's circumstances

Dealing with the Paperwork

No matter what type of planner your family decides to use, you will always have a certain amount of paperwork that needs to be managed: mail, flyers, invitations, directions, concert tickets. Having an easy-to-use method for handling all of this paper can save your family many hours and much frustration.

note EZ Pocket Home-Date Organizer, shown in Figure 2.2. Suggested retail: $32.95. Website: www.ezpocket.com

A device that provides you with a compartment for each day of the month will allow you to sort and retrieve all the pieces of paper that you'll need again soon. These are the items that you'll need in the short term, so you don't need to take the time to put them in file folders where they might be forgotten—you know, out-of-sight, out-of-mind. On the other hand, you know how easily tickets to an event can get lost in a stack of papers and how frantic you get if you're running a little late and have to start rummaging around for them. You can put them where you'll find them in an instant if you use a product such as the EZ Pocket Home-Date Organizer, illustrated in Figure 2.2.

Literature sorters, such as the one shown in Figure 2.3, are great if you're having trouble keeping one family member's mail and papers separate from another's. Give each member an in-slot for the day's mail and other information he needs to act on. Have an out-slot for outgoing mail. Some members might want their own out-slot for things such as signed permission slips that they need to

note Fellowes Smart Stack Literature Organizer with 12 compartments. Suggested retail: $69.95. Website: www.fellowes.com

take back to school. You can get a jump on bill paying by making sure that all bills that come in the mail are immediately put in a separately designated slot. These sorters are very versatile, so you can customize them to fit whatever circumstances are unique to your family.

FIGURE 2.2
This over-the-door canvas organizer lets you easily store and retrieve the papers you'll need for every day of the month.

FIGURE 2.3
Literature sorters are great for keeping papers separated and in easy reach. They are available with 12, 24, 36, or more slots, which can be labeled.

Chapter Summary

In this chapter, you learned how to set up your planner, whether it's a hard-copy or an electronic one. Then you learned how to take information and put it into your planner so that your entire family will be aware of what's going on. And, finally, you saw how to make sure the right information is available for each family member so that she can do her part to keep the schedule running smoothly.

Before leaving this chapter, use the following checklist to make sure you haven't missed a critical step in organizing your family's schedule.

- ❏ Find a "home" for your planner that gives everyone easy access.
- ❏ Enter current information into your planner as a foundation.
- ❏ Teach everyone in the family how the new system works.
- ❏ Decide how each person will take his information with him.
- ❏ Get the accessories you need to support the system.

With a little refinement in the way you go about scheduling your family's time, you'll be able to undertake everything your family needs and wants to do without feeling harried. So, next we're going to take a look at the techniques you'll need to make sure that an activity which should take an hour doesn't end up taking two.

Creating an Activity Schedule

3

"It took me twice as long as I thought it would!" "I thought we'd be home two hours ago." Do these expressions sound familiar? So often our schedules get turned upside down because we haven't allocated enough time to the things we're going to do.

"I would have been on time, but I had to stop to put gas in the car." "We'll have to go out to eat because I forgot to take the meat out of the freezer." Often we're thrown off course because we forgot that we needed to take a preliminary step.

"We've taken a lot of great photos of the kids, and someday we'll put them in albums." "Sure, you have clean shirts; they've been in the dryer for two days." Sometimes the last step of an activity just escapes our attention.

Everything we do in life can be divided into three segments: preparing, doing, and wrapping up. If we want to establish a successful schedule for life's activities, we need to make sure that we don't overlook any of these components. In this chapter, you'll learn how to plan for *all* of the time and tasks involved in participating in scheduled activities. You'll learn how to schedule time to get ready to participate, estimate how much time you'll spend on each of the scheduled items, and plan for and accommodate unscheduled events that can throw your schedule off-track. Finally, you'll look at the issue of follow-through; your activity isn't over until all of the necessary wrap-up components are completed, so you'll need to include time for those details in your schedule, as well.

Preparing for an Activity or Event

Some people thrive on anticipation and preparation. They don't have too much trouble handling this part of the scheduling. Other people focus on the event itself and often find themselves running around at the last minute. A smooth-running schedule must allow time for all of the preparatory activity.

You may not be aware of it, but getting ready for even the simplest of activities is really a complex series of decisions and events. Some of them come very naturally to you, so you won't need to schedule all of their details separately. For example, when you set aside a half hour to shower and get dressed in the morning, you probably don't have to break down the process minute-by-minute into all of the following components:

- Take off pajamas.
- Adjust water in shower.
- Lather.
- Rinse.
- Turn off water.
- Dry off.
- Apply deodorant.
- Put on clothes.
- Comb hair.

On the other hand, you may have more success with some other activities if you take the time to schedule their various components. For example, if you've received an invitation to a birthday party that you plan to attend, you'll probably remember to put the party on your calendar. But you should also consider scheduling the following preparatory activities:

- RSVP.
- Buy a present.
- Buy a card.

- Wrap the present; make sure you have

   Wrapping paper.

   Ribbon.

   Tape.

- Select what you'll wear; make sure

   It fits.

   It's clean/pressed/mended.

- Make sure you have

   Transportation to the party.

   Directions to the party.

- Arrange for a babysitter (if necessary).

In general, asking yourself the following questions will go a long way toward making sure that you schedule all the preliminary steps to make the main event happen stress-free:

❑ Do I have the necessary information to do this?

❑ If not, how can I get the information, and how long will it take?

❑ Do I have what I need in terms of tools, equipment, ingredients?

❑ If not, where will I get them, and how long will it take?

❑ Do I need to do anything in advance of the activity?

❑ If yes, when do I have to do these tasks, and how long will they take?

❑ Do other people need to be involved in preparing for this activity?

❑ If yes, when will they be available?

❑ Is there anything else I must do to be ready for this activity?

Participating in the Activity

The second aspect of every scheduled activity is participation in the actual event. As long as you remember to schedule the event at all, you don't have to worry about skipping this phase. Instead, the challenge at this point is to know how much time to allot for the activity.

You may feel that tasks always take longer to complete than you think they should. They may be taking too long for a variety of reasons. Lack of preparation is one reason. But you should be well on your way to conquering this problem after having read the previous section. Another reason is failure to focus. Distractions and interruptions can erode time at an incredible rate. Making sure the task is scheduled and then sticking to working on the task during the scheduled time will help you accomplish your work in a more reasonable amount of time.

Estimating the Time You'll Spend on an Activity

So, how do you decide how much time to block out for a particular activity? Follow these steps:

1. Estimate how much time you would need to complete the task at your absolute top speed with no interruptions.

2. Estimate how long you would need to do it at normal speed with a normal number of interruptions.

3. Add the estimated times together and divide by two.

This formula will give you a number that's longer than the time you will need for many things after you have your schedule well in hand, but it will be a good time frame from which to start.

caution Although you want to set and stick with an efficient schedule, you should be careful not to schedule your time too tightly. Scheduling your activities so that you have to do them at top speed and then rush on to get to the next item on the list will result in the same harried feeling you get from not having planned your schedule at all.

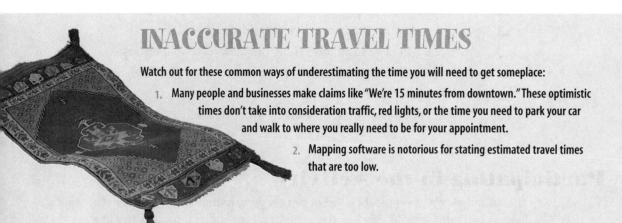

INACCURATE TRAVEL TIMES

Watch out for these common ways of underestimating the time you will need to get someplace:

1. Many people and businesses make claims like "We're 15 minutes from downtown." These optimistic times don't take into consideration traffic, red lights, or the time you need to park your car and walk to where you really need to be for your appointment.

2. Mapping software is notorious for stating estimated travel times that are too low.

Making Good Use of Leftover Time Fragments

Strive to have a pocket of unscheduled time between each scheduled item. This way, you have a built-in cushion for situations in which things don't go quite according to plan—say you get caught in a traffic jam or run into a friend you haven't seen in years—so your stress level will stay low. You can keep a list of small items you can do to fill the gaps if you finish with time to spare.

Here are some suggestions of good items for your fill-in-the-gap list:

- Write a note to a friend.
- Phone a friend.
- Play a game with your child.
- Water your plants.
- Sew a button.
- Read a magazine.
- Clean out the glove box in your car.
- Balance your checkbook.
- Check last night's sports scores.
- Take a walk.

Or, occasionally, you can just reward yourself by putting your feet up for a few minutes.

INTERRUPTIONS

Estimates indicate that the average office worker is interrupted from what she is doing eight times an hour. The average interruption takes 6 minutes from start to finish. That 6 minutes includes the time to switch focus from what she was doing to the interruption, to deal with the interruption, and to return her focus to the original task. This situation is analogous to stopping for a red light: There's the time to decelerate and stop, the actual time while stopped at the red light, and then the time to start and accelerate back up to your original speed. If the office worker does nothing to reduce these interruptions, that means 48 minutes out of every hour are spent on something other than the primary task. With only 12 minutes an hour being spent on what she set out to accomplish, it's a matter of simple mathematics to figure that a one-hour job will take five hours to complete.

Following Through After the Activity or Event

The last component of any activity—the wrapping up, cleaning up, putting things away, enjoying the accomplishment part—is the one most overlooked and neglected by people who tend to be disorganized. These people's creative tendencies find the last step boring or superfluous. They want to get on to exciting new projects.

But this last step is critical to a smooth-running schedule and a less frazzled life. Suitcases need to be unpacked; paint brushes must be cleaned; library books (and especially rented videos) must be returned. And nothing will destroy the benefit of a restful vacation quicker than having to head back to work the next day and face a full schedule of meetings and report deadlines along with the post-vacation pile-up of mail, phone messages, and email.

If you're pressed for time, you certainly won't see as much urgency in cleaning up as you will in moving on. But if you take the time to wrap things up, you'll find you can live in the present with a good outlook to the future instead of feeling as though nothing is ever quite accomplished. Don't lose sight of your reason for wanting to organize your family's schedule: to reduce your stress and increase your enjoyment of life. If you won't go the final step without a reminder, then schedule the wrap-up as a separate item on your to do list.

In general, asking yourself the following questions will go a long way toward making sure that you schedule all the follow-up steps to wrap up an activity so that you feel satisfied and don't have a nagging feeling of incompleteness:

- ❏ Is there anything to clean up?
- ❏ If yes, when will you clean it, and how long will this task take?
- ❏ Is there anything to put away?
- ❏ If yes, when will you put it away, and how long will this task take?
- ❏ Are there any follow-up activities, such as having photos developed or writing thank-you notes?
- ❏ If yes, when will you do them, and how long will they take?
- ❏ Do any other people need to be involved in the wrap-up of this activity?
- ❏ If yes, when will they be available?
- ❏ Is there anything else you can do to make this activity more complete?

note The highly acclaimed Montessori instruction method teaches how to do things by breaking down tasks into their smallest components.

ORGANIZING FOR EVERYONE'S LEVEL OF DETAIL

As we've explained, every task you do has three parts to it: setting it up, doing it, and wrapping it up. For some people this entire three-step process is seen as one seamless event. These are the people who never leave the board sitting out after the game is over because, to them, putting the pieces away is all part of playing the game. These people are never left with paint-encrusted brushes or unpacked suitcases either. If some of the people in your family have brains that work this way, you should be aware that you can allow them to maintain their schedules in a less-detailed way.

For other people, playing the game ends when someone has won. Putting the board away is an unrelated event. For these people, other events unto themselves include cleaning the paint brushes after the garage is painted and unpacking suitcases after a vacation. If some of the people in your family have brains that work this way, you should be aware that they will need to maintain schedules in much more detail.

There's no universal right or wrong amount of detail in a person's schedule. It's all about what works for each individual. As long as your family members are aware of individual differences as they organize the family's schedule, they will be able to do their part to keep family life running smoothly.

Things You'll Need

- ☐ Comprehensive activity list
- ☐ Your answers to the questions listed in previous sections of this chapter
- ☐ Paper
- ☐ Pen/pencil

Creating and Using To Do Lists

You probably make lists of things to do all the time. But do they serve their purpose, or are you often left at the end of the day with a list of things you didn't do? To create an effective to do list, you need to have an understanding of everything you want to accomplish within a certain time frame. Parts II and III of this book will show you how to create a comprehensive activity list for your family. Then, for each item on that list, you need to make a separate list of all of the component tasks involved in completing that item. You can make that list by following these steps:

1. State the main activity.

2. List everything that needs to be done to prepare for the task. Use the questions listed earlier in the chapter to help you.

3. List everything that needs to be done to complete the task. Use the questions listed in the last section to help you.

Your list doesn't have to be a numbered series of items going down a page. As an alternative to writing a list, you can draw an activity map, such as the one shown in Figure 3.1.

FIGURE 3.1

You can substitute an activity map for a list. Here, all of the preparatory items are on spokes above the main event, and all of the follow-up items are below it.

Just breaking down the activity into its components isn't enough, though. Each component has to be completed in its correct order, so the next step in using your list is to put the steps in sequence. If you've made a list, you can assign each line a number or numbers indicating your planned chronology, as shown in Figure 3.2. If you prefer more visual tools, such as the activity map, then you may also prefer sequencing the steps by using a timeline, as shown in Figure 3.3.

FIGURE 3.2

After you've listed everything you need to do, number the items in the order you'll do them. If you plan to do two items at the same time, they both get the same number. If an item requires two steps, then it gets two numbers.

3		buy present
4		buy card
6		wrap present
4		wrapping paper
4		ribbon
X		tape
X		outfit
7		wash blouse
10	8	dryclean suit
5		buy new shoes
2		internet directions
9		gas in car
11		take camera, gift, directions
12		develop photos
13		send photos
14		photos in album
1		RSVP

FIGURE 3.3

Placing all of the items from your activity map onto a timeline allows you to see the sequence in which you need to do them.

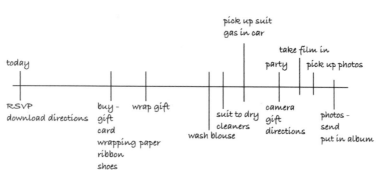

After you've put the steps in order, you still have one more phase to go in the planning process. That's to schedule the steps into your planner. Only after each step has been assigned a time slot during which it will be performed have you succeeded in establishing a plan that, if carried out, will get the job done in an orderly and unharried way.

DEFRAGMENTING YOUR TIME

In our example of the friend's birthday party, you may have noticed that some items were grouped together during the sequencing phase of the planning. They were grouped together strategically to make more efficient use of time. We mentioned earlier how an interruption takes time not just for the interruption itself but also for the time required to shift attention to the interruption and then the time needed to shift attention back to the original task. Everything you do has a wind-up time and a wind-down time.

Sometimes these chunks of time are barely noticeable—for example, every time you sit down to do desk work and then shift away to do something else. In our example, you can see that we grouped replying to the invitation and getting the driving directions together, even though the directions wouldn't be needed for quite some time. However, because they were both desk activities, there is a small savings of time involved in approaching the activities this way.

Sometimes these chunks of time are obvious—for example, in the case of errands, where you have to spend the time to drive to the shopping center and to drive back from the shopping center. One trip, obviously, takes less time than two trips. That's why in the example we've lumped the shopping together as much as possible.

Why, you may ask, if this consumption of extra time is so obvious, don't we avoid it naturally? The answer is that sometimes we do. But sometimes lack of organization gets in our way. In other words, the more disorganized we are, the less efficient we are. The less efficient we are, the more disorganized we become. So, we get caught in a spiral of disorganization. One reason you may not group your errands together is that you don't remember that some of the errands need to be done. This reason is the result of a failure to plan properly. Another reason is that you may have scheduled your activities too tightly, so although you may have time to get to the dry cleaners to pick up your dress, you don't have enough time to also stop at the drugstore for toothpaste. This means that because you don't have 10 minutes to buy toothpaste now, buying toothpaste tomorrow will take you 30 minutes. To get a greater appreciation of how defragmenting your tasks can save you both time and money, compare the two scenarios in Table 3.1.

Table 3.1   Buying Milk and Cereal

Scenario 1: Two Trips	Time	$	Scenario 2: One Trip	Time	$
Drive to store (avg. 3 miles)	10	1.00	Drive to store (avg. 3 miles)	10	1.00
Walk through ice cream aisle to milk	2		Walk through ice cream aisle to milk	2	
(Stop and get ice cream)	1	2.50	(Stop and get ice cream)	1	2.50
Pick up milk	1	2.00	Pick up milk	1	2.00
Walk through cookie aisle to checkout	1		Walk through cereal aisle to checkout	1	
(don't get cookies because you got ice cream)					
Wait in checkout line	3		Pick up cereal	1	3.00
Check out	4		Wait in checkout line	3	
Drive home	10	1.00	Check out	4	
Drive to store	10	1.00	Drive home	10	1.00
Walk directly to cereal aisle	2		**Total**	**33**	**9.50**
Pick up cereal	1	3.00			
Walk through cookie aisle to checkout	1				
(Stop and get cookies)	1	2.50			
Wait in checkout line	3				
Check out	4				
Drive home	10	1.00			
Total	**64**	**14.00**			

Organizing your schedule pays. This example shows how you can save 31 minutes of your time and $4.50 of your money by planning ahead and scheduling your time wisely so that you make one trip to buy milk and cereal instead of two trips. If you eliminated one trip to the store every week, you'd gain more than 26 hours and save about $230 a year.

Chapter Summary

In this chapter, you learned the details of breaking down an event into its components and putting them in your schedule in a way that makes efficient use of your time. Understanding this skill, coupled with what you learned in the previous chapters about selecting and setting up a family scheduling tool, gives you all of the theory you need to know to organize your family's schedule.

Before leaving this chapter, use the following checklist to make sure you haven't missed a critical step in organizing your family's schedule.

- ☐ Select an activity on your list of things to do.
- ☐ Make a list of everything you need to do to prepare for the activity.
- ☐ Make a list of everything you'll need to do to wrap up after the activity.
- ☐ Create a timeline of all of the activities you've listed.
- ☐ Assign each item a time slot in your planner, grouping similar items to improve your efficiency.

In the next part, we'll explore the activities and situations that pertain to your family in particular. Then we'll look at how to apply the theory you've learned to the scheduling challenges you face every day.

Part II

Life's Activities

Dealing with the Necessities of Life

4

A t the mention of organizing family schedules, the first thing that pops into people's minds is usually activities such as soccer games and dance lessons. That's not so different from when we think of a birthday cake, and our first thoughts are of icing and candles. Yes, icing and candles make the cake special; and soccer games and dance lessons make life special. But, in either case, there is a base on which the special features need to be built. In the case of organizing your family's schedule, that base must be a solid schedule of life's necessities—taking care of your family and your home.

We all have the same amount of time: 168 hours a week. How we allocate and manage that time determines how satisfying our lives will be. Even if you have lots of obligations that take up huge chunks of your time, you can find ways to manipulate your schedule so that you have more time and energy for life's fun stuff, too. This chapter will show you how to do that.

To do list

- ❑ Block out time for earning money
- ❑ Schedule time to take care of family needs
- ❑ Schedule time for pet care
- ❑ List and schedule home maintenance tasks

Setting Aside Time for the Basics

If taking care of the basics sounds tedious to you, remember that a little time invested to make your family's basic life run smoothly will allow everyone to enjoy the special activities even more. In this section, you'll learn how to build a schedule that accommodates the demands of your job, along with the necessities of caring for your family, your pets, and your home.

Things You'll Need

- ❑ An 8 1/2- by 11-inch spiral notebook
- ❑ Your family's planner
- ❑ Pen/pencil
- ❑ Calculator
- ❑ Calendar

Making Money

Unless you're independently wealthy, making sure you have enough money to feed and shelter your family has to be a top priority. Making enough money and managing the money you make both come into play as you work to establish your family's financial well-being. And every decision you make about your family's financial situation has an effect on your family's schedule.

Your Primary Income

When you have a job, a certain amount of your time is no longer under your control. You need to subtract the hours you're required to be at work from the 168 hours with which you started. If you work a 40-hour/week job, that means you're down to

128 hours. Obviously, if you work a longer or shorter week, then you need to adjust accordingly. Commuting time and lunch time become somewhat restricted as well, although a little later we'll look at some ways to make these times more productive for you personally.

KIDS AND SCHOOL

For your school-age children, attending school is their work. The school sets the days and hours that your children must be there, and you need to block out that time on their schedules. Just as the time your boss expects you to be at work is not yours, the time the school district expects your children to be at school is not theirs.

Supplemental Jobs

In today's economy, many families feel that they cannot make ends meet on just one salary. So, the one adult in the family takes on multiple jobs, both adults in the family have jobs, or both adults take on more than one job. Unfortunately, multiple jobs often result in a case of diminishing returns; the adults work longer hours with little or no increase in the family's disposable income.

To avoid this pitfall of diminishing returns, when evaluating a second—or third or fourth—job, you should look at it from a couple of angles. First, consider the reason for the supplemental employment. Ask yourself the following questions:

1. Am I taking this job because I really enjoy the work?
2. Is it important for me to have this job so I can stay current in my chosen field or so I can return to my career when the kids are grown?
3. Will this job help me set an example for my children about our family's work ethic or the ability for everyone to be gainfully employed?
4. Am I taking this job because the family needs more money?

If you answered "Yes" to one or more of the first three questions but answered "No" to question number 4, then this job may really be more of an enrichment activity (see Chapter 6, "Participating in Enrichment Activities") than a source of supplemental income.

If you answered "Yes" only to question number 4, then you need to evaluate your situation in light of the example set forth in Table 4.1.

Table 4.1 How Much Money Are You Keeping from Your Family's Second Income?

Income/Expense	Amount	Balance
Earnings		
40 hours/week × 50 weeks = 2,000 hours @ $13/hour	26,000	26,000
Taxes (federal, state, local)		
25%	6,500	19,500
Day care		
$150/week × 50 weeks	7,500	12,000
Work clothes		
4 new outfits/year @ $350 apiece	1,400	10,600
Dry cleaning for work clothes		
$10/week × 50 weeks	500	10,100
Extra lunches out		
1/week @ $10 apiece × 50 weeks	500	9,600
Extra family dinners eaten out		
3/week @ $50 apiece × 50 weeks	7,500	2,100
Gasoline		
10 miles/day × 250 days @$2/gallon, 25 mpg	200	1,900
House cleaning service		
$50/week × 52 weeks	2,600	(700)

If, instead of taking this second job, you stayed home and spent one day a week cleaning the house, at the end of the year, you'd come out $700 and 1,600 hours ahead.

Your income and expenses will vary from the example, but you should never take extra employment without first doing a cost/benefit analysis of the situation.

Trimming Expenses

You've just seen how added expenses can wipe out a large sum of money fairly quickly. But you've also seen how to save $700. And, back in Table 3.1 of Chapter 3, "Creating an Activity Schedule," you saw how to save another $230, all while saving substantial amounts of time as well. So, while saving money is not the primary topic of this book, it's important for you to realize that trimming expenses and having more free time often go hand in hand. With that in mind, you should consider these other ways that good scheduling can help you trim your expenses:

- Save gasoline, wear and tear on your car, and impulse purchasing by consolidating errands.

- Pay your bills on time and eliminate late-payment penalties.

- Eliminate meals eaten out because of lack of meal planning.

- Maintain your house on a regular schedule and avoid costly repair bills.

- Incorporate exercise into your other activities and save gym fees (see Table 4.5).

> **note** The 5-in-1 Minimi$er Organizer combines an activity calendar, menu planner, grocery list, budget, and reward system on one 11- by 17-inch page per month. Suggested retail: $14.95. Website: www.onlineorganizing.com

Investing Your Savings

Now that you've created some savings, it's important that you don't just let them sit idly or, worse, get absorbed into your regular spending without being noticed. Be sure you take the important first step by incorporating money management as an activity on your schedule. So, when you start to make your to do lists later in this chapter, don't forget to include time to review your finances and make some investment choices. Remember, the harder your money works for you, the less hard you'll have to work and the more time you'll have for the fun things in life.

Caring for the People in Your Family

If you didn't care about the people in your family, you wouldn't be reading this book. And yet, so often, when we work on putting together a family schedule, we completely forget about the essentials needed to take care of the people in our family. As we mentioned before, we get so caught up in the extra, special activities that we overlook the basics that are crucial to health and happiness. We'll get to the extras later, but for now let's make sure we cover the basics.

Every person needs time in his schedule for the following:

- Taking care of personal hygiene

- Eating

- Exercising

- Sleeping

- Socializing (see Chapter 7, "Planning Other Fun Stuff")

Now is a good time to take out your spiral notebook and start making some lists. Each family member should have a personalized list of needs because needs vary based on age, gender, personal preference, and personal circumstance. For example, someone who plays soccer as an enrichment activity (see Chapter 6) will need to schedule less exercise time than someone who chooses chess club for enrichment. For each list, you should also indicate how much time each item will take and how often each item needs to be done. Figure 4.1 shows an example of the beginning of a personal needs list.

Jane		
shower	daily	20 min.
bubble bath	once a week	45 min.
dentist	2 times/yr	1 1/2 hrs
haircut	every month	1 hour
aerobics	3 times/wk	45 min.

Just as when you have a paid job you must block out from your schedule the chunk of time you must be at work, you also must block out a huge chunk of your time for sleep. Individual sleep needs vary, but Table 4.2 will give you an idea of how much time to allow each person in your family for sleep.

Many people shave more and more time off their sleep block because they think this is the only part of their schedule in which they can get time to do the things they don't get around to doing otherwise. But by depriving yourself of sleep, you actually reduce the amount of productive time you have while you're awake because insufficient sleep

- Diminishes your energy and performance during the day
- Reduces your ability to concentrate
- Impairs your memory
- Depletes your immune system
- Reduces your motivation

 It doesn't take much sleep to make a huge impact.

Consider these facts:

* Sleeping one hour longer at night generally boosts your alertness by 25%.

* One night's sleep debt reduces the time to reach total exhaustion by 11%.

* In the four days after we lose an hour to switch to daylight savings time, there is a 7% increase in accidental deaths compared to the one-week periods before and after that time!

- Makes you indecisive
- Causes you to lose your sense of humor

In other words, what you lose in time by getting the sleep you need, you make up in increased productivity when you're awake.

caution Don't wake up early to work out. The stress from the sleep loss cancels the benefits of the exercise!

Table 4.2   Average Sleep Needs Per Day by Age

Age	Hours
Newborns	10–19
2–12 months	14–15
12–18 months	13–15
18 months–3 years	12–14
3–5 years	11–13
5–12 years	9–11
12–20 years	8–10
Adults	7–9

Source: *The National Sleep Foundation; www.sleepfoundation.org*

WHAT DOES YOUR BRAIN DO WHILE YOU'RE ASLEEP?

Most people are familiar with the notion that while they sleep their bodies repair themselves, and most people would not be surprised to learn that during sleep the brain stockpiles neurotransmitters—norepinephrine and serotonin—that it will need for attention and learning when they're awake.

Most people also think that while they sleep their brains rest. Not so. Your brain is often more active when you're asleep than when you're awake. It's busy making sure it stays organized:

❋ It grows neural connections to hold memories, analogous to your going out and buying a file cabinet and other filing supplies.

❋ It goes through its long-term memory storage and decides to forget some things, the same way you'd go through a filing cabinet and throw out old papers that were once important but that you no longer need to keep.

✳ It frees up capacity for new long-term memories, just as cleaning out your file cabinets gives you room to file newer papers.

✳ While it's going through your long-term memory, your brain is also strengthening your memory of important stored events, just as running across old papers may remind you that you have them.

✳ Your brain discards some short-term memories instead of moving them to long-term memory, similar to your throwing out junk mail after a quick review.

✳ Your brain takes the new memories it's going to keep and which it stored temporarily in its hippocampal zone and moves them systematically into the brain's neocortal zone, similar to your sorting through piles of paper and filing documents where they belong.

In other words, getting enough sleep is directly related to your brain's ability to manage information. If you don't get enough sleep, your brain will become frantic, looking around for misplaced information the same way you become frantic looking around for misplaced papers if you don't take enough time to put them in their proper place.

Caring for the Pets in Your Family

People aren't the only ones whose needs you must consider. Family pets come along with their own list of care requirements. If you are still at the stage of deciding whether to get a pet or what kind of pet to get, then you should choose responsibly by considering where you have time in your family's schedule.

Of course, the place to begin your decision process is in figuring out why you want a pet:

- For protection
- As a companion
- To teach your children responsibility
- To motivate you to go for a walk every day

But you also should consider how much time your family will have to devote to a pet and whether the pet's schedule will match yours. A large dog that needs to be walked three times a day will take a minimum of 312 hours of care a year. And someone will have to be available mid-day to take the dog for a walk. Plus, don't forget the need for extra housecleaning that a dog will generate. And if your family plans to travel without the dog, then kenneling becomes an issue as well.

On the other end of the spectrum are goldfish. They're not warm and cuddly, but they're still enjoyable (and calming). If you put them in a tank with a good filter, your annual time commitment to feeding and maintenance will come out to only about 14 hours a year.

In terms of scheduling, you'll need to make a list for each of your pets similar to the lists you made for each family member. Figure 4.2 shows an example.

tip Estimated first year costs for pets run between $75 and $1,500, so be sure to research both the time and money aspects of a new pet carefully.

FIGURE 4.2
You'll also need a list of each pet's needs, along with frequencies and time estimates.

Fido		
take for walk	3 times/day	45 min. total
veterinarian	2 times/yr	2 hours
bath	4 times/yr	2 hrs
feed	daily	10 minutes
groom	weekly	20 min.

Maintaining Your Home

Now it's time to make a list of everything that needs to be done concerning the care of your home. This list will be very long, but we'll show you how to break it down into manageable pieces and how to slot those pieces into your family's schedule. By making a thorough list now, you'll ensure that little details don't "fall through the cracks" and leave you frantically running around dealing with routine items that have suddenly become urgent.

Listing Tasks Room by Room

The easiest way to make your list is for you to spend a few minutes in each room of your home. Look around and write down anything you can think of that needs to be done with anything in the room. For example, if you're in the living room and you have a fireplace, you might come up with a list that includes the items in Figure 4.3. The idea right now is to make a completely comprehensive list. You don't need to think about categorizing it or sorting it out; that will come later. Don't be discouraged if your list takes up several pages; some households will easily have more than 500 entries on their lists.

FIGURE 4.3
You'll need a list of
all of your home
maintenance items
before you begin
assigning them time
slots in your family's
schedule.

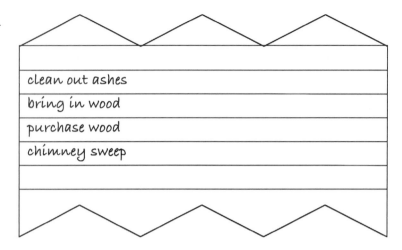

Assigning Task Frequency

When you think your list is complete—you can
always go back and add items you forgot—it is
time to assign each item a frequency, as shown in
Figure 4.4. Don't get too detail-oriented here.
Whenever sensible, try to limit your selection to
the following choices:

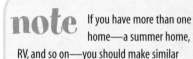

note If you have more than one
home—a summer home,
RV, and so on—you should make similar
lists for each one as well.

- Daily (examples: open mail, put away toys)
- Weekly (examples: take out trash, pay bills)
- Monthly (examples: file papers, wash car)
- Quarterly (examples: turn mattresses, get oil changed)
- Yearly (examples: clean chandelier, file tax returns)
- One time only (examples: get new bathroom sink faucet, plant tree in front
  yard)

If you need to do something more than once a day, then list each instance as a separate item. For example, if you need to run your dishwasher both in the morning
after breakfast and in the evening after dinner, then list the task like this:

- Run dishwasher—morning (daily)
- Run dishwasher—evening (daily)

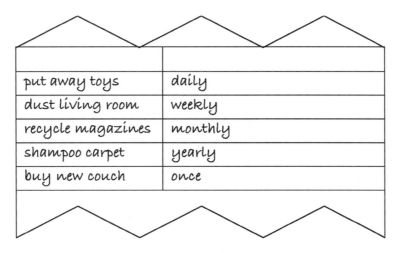

FIGURE 4.4
The second step in creating your master list is to assign each item a frequency.

put away toys	daily
dust living room	weekly
recycle magazines	monthly
shampoo carpet	yearly
buy new couch	once

Deciding how often to do something can be tricky. We all tend to want to assign an ideal frequency to each task. For example, maybe you were taught that bed sheets should be changed every week. On the other hand, if your family's schedule currently is out of control, you may not be changing the sheets more often than once a month. At least in the beginning of your new organizing endeavors, consider whether you can feel comfortable—and still better off than now—by compromising and assigning this task a frequency of every two weeks.

Scheduling Daily, Weekly, and Monthly Tasks

The next step is to decide the best time to accomplish each task. The easiest way to do this is to start with the items that you've decided to do on a weekly basis. Assign each of these items a specific day of the week. Some assignments will be obvious; for example, you take out the trash on the day your neighborhood has trash collection. When it comes to other items, you'll want to have an outline in place to help make your decisions easier. To do that, designate a focus for each day of the week. (Remember how in Chapter 3 we discussed the increased efficiency of grouping errands together?) As a starting point, you can focus one day each week as follows:

1. Errands
2. Paperwork
3. Heavy housework
4. Light housework
5. Projects
6. Free day (see Chapter 7)
7. Family day (see Chapters 5 & 7)

Next, deal with the items your family will do every month. Once again, you'll use your daily focus plan to decide which day of the week will work best. For example, if you're going to have your car washed once a month, you'll assign it to your errand day. On the other hand, if someone in the family is going to wash the car, that chore might get assigned to the light housework day. If your family makes an activity out of it—complete with water fight—family day is a valid option.

Because you'll be doing monthly things only once every four or five weeks, you should also distribute your monthly tasks throughout the month by assigning them a week, such as "first Monday of the month" or "third Tuesday of the month." Avoid listing anything for the fifth week of the month because no months contain a complete fifth week. Figure 4.5 gives you an idea of how your list will start to look.

> **note** If you work in an office, you can try the same daily focus technique at work, having one day of each week focused on the following:
>
> 1. Planning/projects
> 2. Meetings
> 3. Correspondence
> 4. Phone calls
> 5. Flexible day

FIGURE 4.5

Each day of the week has a focus, and you schedule the items on your to do list according to that plan.

dust living room	weekly	Monday
pay bills	weekly	Thurs.
sweep garage floor	monthly	2nd Mon.
return library books	weekly	Tues.
grocery shopping	weekly	Tues.
file papers	monthly	3rd Thurs.

Scheduling Annual Tasks

After you've set up your plan for daily, weekly, and monthly home maintenance requirements, you should complete the plan by dealing with the items that your family needs to do on a yearly basis. Much the same way that you established a focus for each day of the week, you should now establish a focus for each month of the year. Your plan might look something like this:

- January—attic
- February—paperwork, taxes
- March—bathrooms
- April—basement
- May—yard
- June—garage, car
- July—bedrooms
- August—vacation (see Chapter 7)
- September—kitchen
- October—family room
- November—living and dining rooms
- December—holidays (see Chapter 5, "Celebrating Special Occasions")

Be sure to consider the rhythm of your family and your local weather conditions when putting together your monthly focus plan. For example, it's far better to work on cleaning out the closets in your children's bedrooms in July when they are home for the summer. On the other hand, cleaning out a hot attic in July really is not a very appealing—or healthy—idea.

With your monthly plan, you can spread the rest of the items on your list throughout the year. To do that, go back through your list and write the appropriate month next to each of the remaining items. You can use the examples in Figure 4.6 as a guide.

FIGURE 4.6
Using a monthly focus plan enables you to distribute tasks throughout the year in an organized way.

master bedrm closet	yearly	July
kids' bedrm closet	yearly	July
wash bedrm curtains	yearly	July
clean behind stove	yearly	September
change furnace filter	yearly	April
polish chandelier	yearly	November

Estimating Times for Tasks

To be able to create a schedule that will actually work, you also need to have in mind just how long each item on your list will take to accomplish. Now you can put to work the skills you learned in Chapter 3 for analyzing the components of each task and estimating the time needed to complete them. You can also refer to Table 4.3 for some fairly standard time estimates.

note Keep in mind that Table 4.3 does not represent a complete list of common chores because some tasks have no standard times. Evening meal preparation and cleanup are good examples. Some people cook ahead for the whole week, others make simple meals in the microwave, others cook more elaborate meals that require more cleanup. Your own habits will help you fill in the gaps in the list of chores in this table.

Table 4.3 Common Chores with Frequencies and Time Estimates

Chore	Frequency	Time to Complete (in Minutes)
Make bed	daily	2
Load dishwasher	daily	20
Empty dishwasher	daily	5
Go through mail	daily	20
Clear up clutter (per room)	daily	2
Wash laundry (per load)	weekly	10
Dry laundry (per load)	weekly	5
Fold laundry (per load)	weekly	15
Put away laundry (per load)	weekly	5
Dust lightly (per room)	weekly	5
Vacuum (per room)	weekly	5
Clean a bathroom	weekly	25
Take out trash	weekly	10
Water houseplants	weekly	5
Pay bills/deskwork	weekly	30
Plan menus/make grocery list	weekly	15
Shop for groceries	weekly	90
Put gas in car	weekly	10

Table 4.3   Continued

Chore	Frequency	Time to Complete (in Minutes)
Dust thoroughly (per room)	monthly	20
File papers	monthly	15
Turn mattress	quarterly	10
Change car oil	quarterly	30
Clean/replace furnace filter	yearly	15
Wash windows (per room)	yearly	30
Clean behind kitchen appliances	yearly	60
Clean chandelier	yearly	60
Clean out a closet	yearly	90
Clean out medicine cabinet	yearly	15

So, continue with your master list and go through and place a time estimate beside each entry, as shown in Figure 4.7.

FIGURE 4.7
You'll be able to put together a more realistic schedule after you estimate how much time is needed to complete each item on your list.

go through mail	daily		20 min.
grocery shopping	weekly	Tues.	2 hours
sweep garage floor	monthly	2nd Mon.	15 min.
clean behind stove	yearly	September	45 min.
put away toys	daily		15 min.
dust living room	weekly	Mon.	20 min.

SCHEDULING MULTIPART TASKS

When making your time estimates, remember to include time for the setup and wrap-up phases, too. If you think it's unlikely that all three phases will be completed without interruption by the same family member, then consider splitting the task and listing it as two or three separate tasks. For example, you may have a weekly item on your list called "grocery shopping." The setup phase involves creating a grocery shopping list. The actual task is going to the grocery store, buying the items on the list, and bringing them home. The wrap-up phase requires the groceries to be put away. You must decide whether you are more comfortable listing this as one item:

Shop for groceries	weekly	Tuesday	2 hrs.

or as three items:

Make grocery list	weekly	Monday	25 min.
Shop for groceries	weekly	Tuesday	1 hr. 15 min.
Put away groceries	weekly	Tuesday	20 min.

Dividing Your Master List into Time-Specific Lists

Your master list is now complete! Don't make the mistake, though, of thinking that a master list is the same as a schedule. You still have a few more steps to go before you will have created a master schedule. The next step to success will be for you to take your master list and split it into 20 separate lists. Don't worry; you've already done the groundwork, so this phase will be quick and easy.

Turn to a new page in your spiral notebook and copy from your master list all of the items you've indicated your family will do every day. Then create seven lists—one for each day of the week—and transfer your weekly and monthly items to them. Next, make 12 more lists—one for each month—and transfer your yearly household maintenance tasks. You'll end up with the three different types of lists that are represented in Figure 4.8.

Making Sure It All Adds Up

You may have noticed that you have a huge amount of stuff to do. Before you get totally overwhelmed, it's time for a reality check. Each person gets 24 hours in a day. You must subtract from that a minimum of 8 hours for sleep, leaving 16 hours. If you're talking about someone who is working a 40-hour/week job, then five days a week his daily discretionary time is reduced to 8 hours, before you even take into account commuting time and personal care time. If you're talking about a toddler, then you don't even need to begin calculating her discretionary time because the truth is, she's not going to contribute in any significant way to accomplishing any of the tasks you've put on your master list; even if she's helping, you'll have to be next to her every step of the way.

Daily	
put away toys	20 min.
load dishwasher	15 min.
empty dishwasher	5 min.
go through mail	20 min.

Monday —heavy housework	
dust	1 hr.
vacuum	30 min.
clean bathroom	50 min.
mop rec. room floor	30 min.
scrub kitchen floor	1 hr.

March —bathrooms		
clean out medicine cab.	2nd Wed.	30 min.
wash shower curtains	3rd Mon.	30 min.
wash master bath walls	3rd Mon.	50 min.
wash guest bath walls	4th Mon.	40 min.
buy new towels	1st Tues.	1 hr.

So, what do you do if it's obvious that the things you have on your to do list are going to take more time than you have? First, look to see whether the situation can be resolved simply by rearranging the list. For example, maybe you have a lot more to do on a yearly basis in your bedrooms than you do in your kitchen. If that's the case, you could divide the bedroom work between two months and double-up the kitchen with another light month. If, on the other hand, your time estimates simply add up to way more hours than there are in a year, you'll have to consider some other alternatives. In fact, you should consider those alternatives in any event because they are all designed to let you accomplish more in less time. We'll discuss these methods in the next section.

To do list

- ☐ Determine how you might use your time more effectively
- ☐ Find ways to be more efficient in the way you tackle tasks
- ☐ Learn to choose multipurpose tasks
- ☐ Decide when it's best to hire outside help

Increasing Your Productivity

There is a lot of talk in the business world about the difference between being efficient and being effective. The same principles apply to running a family. Here are our basic definitions of these important terms:

- Being *efficient* means getting something done by expending the least amount of time, energy, and money.
- Being *effective* means doing things that really matter.
- Being *productive* means putting together the right combination of efficiency and effectiveness so that you spend your time, energy, and money only on things that matter, you accomplish everything that does matter, and you do so by expending the minimum resources required.

So here you are, faced with a daunting to do list of things that seemingly are going to take more time than you have—and we've described only the necessities in life and haven't even begun to address the fun stuff. We need to arm you with the tools to be more productive. Some would say you need to learn to work smarter, not harder.

Being More Effective

Let's start with effectiveness. Are all of the things you think you need to do really necessary? If you can eliminate something from your list entirely, you'll never have to think about scheduling time to do it! You can remove things from your to do list in several ways.

First, make an honest assessment of where you stand today. Do you have things on your master list that you haven't done in years? If you start doing them now, will they really make a positive impact on your family's life?

- If no one really cares if the lawn is edged every week, then you don't need to try to find a half hour every week of the summer to do it. Eliminating that item will save your family 13 hours a year.

- If everyone uses your side door in the winter, then you don't need to shovel the front walk when it snows (unless you're just doing it for the exercise). Not shoveling the walk will probably save you an average of a half hour a week throughout the winter, or about 8 hours a year.

Next, take a closer look at the frequencies you've assigned to various tasks. Can you reduce how often your family needs to do something?

- You may have indicated on your master list that the guest room should be dusted every week. But if the room doesn't get much use and you find that the dust doesn't really start to show until a month has gone by, reduce the frequency from weekly to monthly and save yourself a half hour every month. That's another 6 hours a year.
- Maybe you plan to change your vacuum cleaner bag every month, but it really needs changing only every three months. Those few minutes saved—and the cost of the bags—will start to add up.

Sometimes using new tools or different methods can eliminate a recurring task:

- Forty years ago, people who lived in parts of the country where it snowed in the winter had to change to snow tires each winter and then back to regular tires in the spring. Now, the technology has changed and almost everyone has all-season tires that work better than the specialized tires of the past.
- Flowers blooming in your flower beds all summer are lovely. But if you're pressed for time, you might consider eliminating the job of planting annual flowers every spring by designing a flower bed full of perennial flowers that will bloom in sequence all through the summer and then continue to bloom year after year.

Finally, see whether certain components of necessary tasks can be eliminated. Do some of your activities contain a lot of fluff?

- If you wash the sheets from your bed and then put a different set of sheets on the bed, you'll have to spend five minutes folding the first set and putting it away. If you put the same set—clean, of course—back onto the bed and switched sets only occasionally to make sure the ones in the closet stayed fresh, you'd gain more than 3 hours a year.
- Every morning when you make your bed, maybe you spend an extra minute placing 10 or 15 decorative pillows that you then remove before you get into bed every night. If you don't even go into your bedroom during the day to enjoy the look of the pillows, you can eliminate them and not even notice. That minute per day you'll save adds up to an extra 6 hours of your time a year!

Increasing Your Efficiency

Next, let's talk about being efficient. After you've eliminated all of the unnecessary items from your to do list so that you're being effective, you can still free up a lot more time by doing the remaining items more efficiently.

Sometimes being efficient is about reducing wasted motions:

- You've already seen how you can save a lot of travel time if you consolidate your errands.
- Carrying a watering can around to each plant that needs watering will take you much less time than carrying each plant, one by one, to the sink.

GROCERY LISTS

Efficient and effective grocery shopping can save you countless hours over the alternatives. And productive grocery shopping begins with a good shopping list. A simple system to record items for purchase when they run out or when someone needs a special ingredient for something he'll be cooking is to have one piece of paper or electronic document onto which anyone in the family can add items that need to be purchased. Then whoever is going to do the shopping can just grab the list and go. The big drawback to this system is that the items will be on the list in a random order—the order in which the need arose—making it difficult for the shopper to get everything on the list without crisscrossing his way through the store.

A more efficient system would list the items in the order in which they would come up if the shopper followed a normal route through the aisles. What you'll want to do is make a master grocery list that contains all of the products you've ever bought at the grocery store. Your custom-designed list will differ from the stock lists you can purchase in two ways. First, it will contain only the items that your family uses. Second, you'll list the items in the order in which you'll come to them as you walk an established route through your favorite grocery store.

Begin by taking your spiral notebook with you to the store and walking up and down the aisles as you make your list. Then, when you return home, set up your system in one of the following two ways:

Method one:

1. Make a neat list with a check box in front of each item. After every few items, leave a blank space in case you left out a product or someone in the family wants to try a new item.
2. Make 50 photocopies—a year's supply—of your list.
3. Post the list in the kitchen, and all family members can check off items as they notice the need.
4. The person who goes to the grocery store takes the list with him and replaces it with a new blank list to begin the cycle again.
5. Before you photocopy your list each year, update it to include new items and adjust for any rearranging of stock on the store shelves.

Method two:

1. Type the list into a computer document.

2. Designate a place in the kitchen—a blank piece of paper, a dry-erase board, an electronic device—where family members can record items to be purchased.

3. Before leaving for the grocery store, the person doing the shopping will delete all of the items on the computer list except the ones that are needed and print out the modified list. Now the person shopping will have a list only of what's needed, which creates more focus—less wasted time and fewer impulse purchases—at the store.

4. The shopper should be careful not to save the changes to the master document because you'll want the full master list available for modification before each shopping trip.

5. Update the master list as needed to include new items and adjust for any way the store has rearranged its shelves.

With either method, you can fold the list to form a pocket to hold the coupons you'll want to use on each shopping trip.

Other times, being efficient is about having the right tools:

- Trying to clean your keyboard with a damp cloth instead of a can of compressed air will take you a lot longer—and may even damage your computer.

- Most people can peel a potato much more quickly and with a lot less effort if they use a potato peeler instead of a paring knife.

 A food freezer can increase your efficiency two ways:

* By keeping food fresh so you can buy more at one time and make fewer trips to the store

* By letting you keep a supply of home-made heat-and-serve meals for days when no one has time to cook

 Some special-purpose gadgets actually end up using more of your time than they save. The reason goes back to the principle that each job has three phases.

For example, suppose you want to slice a cucumber. You can slice it in 3 minutes if you use your paring knife. You can slice it in 30 seconds if you use your slicer-dicer gadget. Getting out your knife will take you 10 seconds; getting out your slicer-dicer and setting it up will take you a minute. When you're finished, rinsing your knife and putting it in the dishwasher will take you 15 seconds; washing and drying the gadget, which is not dishwasher-safe, will take you 5 minutes. So, as you can see from Table 4.4, the gadget will save you time only if you need to slice four or more cucumbers.

Table 4.4   Does the Time-Saving Gadget Really Save You Time?

Number of Cucumbers	Time with Knife	Time with Slicer-Dicer
1	2 min. 25 sec.	6 min. 30 sec.
2	4 min. 25 sec.	7 min.
3	6 min. 25 sec.	7 min. 30 sec.
4	8 min. 25 sec.	8 min.
5	10 min. 25 sec.	8 min. 30 sec.

The lesson here: Evaluate time-saving devices based on your particular circumstances.

SETTING UP AN AUTOMATIC WATERING SYSTEM

Setting up an automatic watering system for your garden will require you to make an upfront investment in terms of time and equipment. The dividends it will pay in terms of saved time later—and healthy, lush plants—are well worth the effort.

You'll need

* A soaker hose the length of your flower bed (a soaker hose is a special hose that has tiny holes all along its surface that allow drops of water to seep out and soak into the ground)
* An automatic water timer
* Batteries for the timer

Here's how to set it up:

1. Install the batteries in your timer.
2. Connect the timer to your outdoor faucet.
3. Place the hose lengthwise through the center of the flower bed and connect the hose to the timer.
4. Turn on the water with the timer on the manual setting and adjust the water flow to your satisfaction.
5. Decide at what time(s) of the day you want the bed to be watered and for how long, and set the timer for the desired watering times.

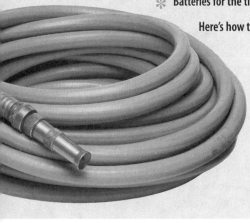

Now your flower bed will be watered automatically without your having to remember to turn the water on or off and without your having to be home (or awake) at the ideal watering time. Your timer will have a manual override in case you want to use the faucet at another time. You always have the option of turning off the system for a day or more if you've had excessive rain.

FIGURE 4.9
An automatic water timer will save you time, and it won't forget to water your garden.

Still another way to increase your efficiency is to make sure you're not letting little pockets of time go unused:

- While you're waiting for something to heat in the microwave, you probably have enough time to sort through the day's mail.

- While you're sitting in your car waiting for your child to come out of her piano lesson, you can write a birthday card to your best friend.

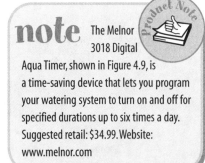

note The Melnor 3018 Digital Aqua Timer, shown in Figure 4.9, is a time-saving device that lets you program your watering system to turn on and off for specified durations up to six times a day. Suggested retail: $34.99. Website: www.melnor.com

SETTING UP A PORTABLE OFFICE

Often you realize that you could be using a few spare minutes to write a letter or pay a few bills, but you can't because you don't have what you need with you. Having a portable office can help.

You'll need

* A portable file box with a pencil tray in the lid
* Six file folders
* A pen
  * A book of postage stamps
  * Your checkbook
    * Your personal address book
    * Stationery, writing paper, or notecards with envelopes
    * Your return address labels (optional)
    * Five paperclips (optional)
    * Mini-stapler (optional)

Here's how to set it up:

1. Label the file folders as follows:

   * **Unpaid bills**—You can put your unpaid bills in this file as you sort your mail every day.
   * **Paid bills**—This is the place where you put the bill stubs after you pay the bills.
   * **Other correspondence**—If you have any nonbill paperwork that requires a response you can prepare away from your computer, you put that here.
   * **Note paper and cards to write**—You should keep a supply of blank note cards to write birthday greetings, condolence notes, and other friendly correspondence; if you buy cards to send, they would go in this file, too.
   * **Checkbook and address list**—Put your checkbook and personal address book in this folder.
   * **Papers to file**—These are papers that you need to move to a more permanent file elsewhere.

2. Place the rest of the supplies in the compartment in the file box lid.

Now your deskwork can move with you without getting separated into segments that tend to get lost or misplaced. You can take your portable office in your car, out on your deck, to the library—anywhere you want.

Doing Two Things at Once

The idea of multitasking has increased in popularity as people have felt more and more pressed for time. However, when you get right down to it, multitasking isn't really about doing more than one thing at a time; it's about switching from one thing to another and back and forth again and again in very rapid succession. If you truly hope to do two things at once, what you want to look for is one activity that accomplishes two purposes. Table 4.5 shows how you can find these activities if you're willing to spend a little time doing some creative thinking.

note The Rubbermaid Office Solutions Simplifile Box Office, shown in Figure 4.10, accommodates letter-size hanging file folders in the base and small supplies in the lid, and is designed for easy portability. Suggested retail: $11.99. Website: www.eldonoffice.com

Product Note

Table 4.5   Accomplishing More by Doing Less

Plan 1	Time	Cost	Plan 2	Time	Cost
1. Hire service to mow lawn for 6 months.		$450	1. Buy push lawnmower.	2 hrs.	$250
2. Join health club for 6 months.		$300	2. Mow lawn for 1 hour a week for 6 months.	26 hrs.	
3. Buy equipment (clothes for health club).	2 hrs.	$150			
4. Drive to and from health club (8 miles) once a week for 6 months.	8 hrs.	$60*			
5. Exercise for 1 hour a week for 6 months.	26 hrs.				
Totals	**36 hrs.**	**$960****		**28 hrs.**	**$250*****

* Also consider the negative impact on the environment.

** This amount might increase in succeeding years.

*** This amount will decrease in succeeding years.

Deciding to Hire Someone Else to Do the Work

You've eliminated everything from your list of necessities that really isn't necessary. You've streamlined the necessary tasks so that you're getting them done in the least amount of time possible. What do you do if it still looks as though you're going to be short of time? Buy more time. You can't increase the number of hours your family has to do things, but you can increase the time available to do the family's chores by hiring someone else to do some of them. Prime candidates on your to do lists include

- Chores that no one in the family enjoys doing
- Chores that no one in the family has the skills to do

Your decision to hire another person to do the work boils down to whether you're more willing or able to undertake the hiring and management of the chore than to actually do the chore—and whether you are willing and able financially to afford hiring someone to do it. The following questionnaire provides you with one method of making those determinations.

Do the Job Yourself or Hire Someone to Do It?

1. Do you have the ability—physical strength and know-how—to do the job?
   If no, go directly to X.

2. How long will doing the job take you? _____ hours.

3. Do you have enough time to do it?
   If no, go directly to X.

4. How much will it cost you to have a professional do the job? $_____.

5. Do you have enough money to hire a professional to do it?
   If no, go directly to Y.

6. How much will the materials and equipment cost if you do it? $_____.

7. Calculate:
   a. Enter your answer from question 4. _____
   b. Enter your answer from question 6. _____
   c. Subtract line b from line a (a – b). _____
   d. Enter your answer from question 2. _____
   e. Divide line c by line d (c ÷ d). _____
   f. Multiply line e by 2 (2 × e.) _____

8. Would you do this job for someone else if he paid you at an hourly rate equal
   to the amount on line f?
   If yes, score 1 point.

9. Can you do this job in less than double the time a professional can? (Refer to
   your answer to question 2.)
   If yes, score 1 point.

10. Is this job something you'll really enjoy doing?
    If yes, score 1 point.

11. If your score is 0 or 1, go to X.

12. If your score is 2 or 3, go to Y.

X. Hire someone.

Y. Do it yourself.

To do list

- ☐ Have each family member fill out the self-assessment questionnaires
- ☐ Determine which checklist format will work best for your family
- ☐ Create your checklists
- ☐ Schedule the items from your checklists into your family's planner

Using Your Lists

In Chapter 1, "Selecting a Planner," you spent a lot of time making sure that you selected a planner that fit your family's style. You need to make similar choices now before you convert the time-specific lists you created earlier in this chapter into checklists. The self-assessment questionnaires in Tables 4.6 and 4.7 will help you determine the best format and configuration for your family's checklists. Have each family member complete both questionnaires. Keep in mind that, in the end, each person will be able to have her own individual checklist that suits her personal style.

As you create your checklists, you can make preliminary assignments of tasks to individual family members based on each person's age and other obligations. In Part III, we'll take a closer look at who's assigned what, and then you may want to make some adjustments to the assignments.

You'll determine where you keep your lists and how you use them based on the formatting option you select. Generally, you'll keep the checklists near your family's planner, although as your family becomes more accustomed to using the schedule, some members will take full responsibility for the location and use of their own checklists. We'll discuss this process more in Part III, as well.

Table 4.6   Handwritten or Typewritten?

	a	b
1. If you are handed a page with both typed text and handwritten text, which text do you read first?		
a. Typed text		
b. Handwritten text		
2. When someone sends you a thank-you note, which do you prefer receiving?		
a. A printed thank-you card		
b. A handwritten note		
3. Do you hesitate to write changes or questions on a printed document?		
a. Yes		
b. No		

If you answered more *a*'s than *b*'s, try using typewritten lists. Conversely, if you answered more *b*'s than *a*'s, try using handwritten lists, even if they are photocopies.

Table 4.7   Indicating a "To Do" Is Done

If you had your choice, which of the following methods would you use to indicate you had completed an item on a checklist?

- Check it off.
- Cross it out/draw a line through it.
- Delete it from the list.
- Highlight it.

The questionnaire in Table 4.6 will help each person decide whether she responds better to words that are typewritten or words that are handwritten. You'll find that by using the kind of printing that carries the most weight in the user's mind, you'll help her to focus on the message being conveyed by the list—that is, what needs to be done. The added focus may be just the boost she needs to actually do the job.

Next, you need to find an efficient way to present your checklists over and over again. After all, you'll need 365 daily checklists, 52 weekly checklists, and 12 monthly checklists a year. Of course, several options are available, each with its own set of plusses and minuses. The following sections discuss these options in more detail.

Things You'll Need

- ❑ Paper
- ❑ Pen/pencil
- ❑ Computer (optional)
- ❑ Printer or photocopy machine
- ❑ Highlighters (optional)

Using Paper Checklists

Paper checklists can be used only once. But you can design a daily checklist with enough check boxes to last a week if you've chosen to check things off rather than to cross them out or highlight them, as shown in Figure 4.11. In a similar manner, you can place a month's worth of weekly checklists on a single page. If you've chosen to use typewritten lists, you can make a master list on your computer and then print off clean copies—modified to include new assignments, if appropriate—as you need them. If your family responds better to handwriting, you can save the time of writing a new list every time you need a fresh copy by making one original and then photocopying it. (The photocopied handwriting will have almost the same force in the user's mind as an original handwritten piece.)

Your ability to make multiple copies of your blank checklists quickly and easily becomes even more important if your family prefers crossing off or highlighting the tasks as they're done. With those methods, if you're using paper checklists, you have no choice but to have a separate list for each day, for each week, and for each month.

caution Some people think that an advantage paper lists have over all of the other list media is that they can keep them to refer back to if they ever want to see what and how their family was doing at any particular time. However, you're making these checklists for only the most routine of tasks—basically chores—so the odds of your ever wanting or needing to look back are slim. Even if you're a family-chronicle fanatic, keeping one blank copy of each form should satisfy your yen to preserve your family's history.

FIGURE 4.11
This daily checklist will last your family an entire week. You can use a checklist like this one with either typewritten or handwritten text. The column that assigns the task to a particular person is optional.

Daily Checklist - Week of 10/17/04									
What to do	**Time**	**Who**	**S**	**M**	**T**	**W**	**T**	**F**	**S**
put away toys	20 min	Dick & Jane	√	√	√				
load dishwasher	15 min	Mom	√	√	√				
empty dishwasher	5 min	Jane	√	√					
go through mail	20 min	Mom	✕	√	√				

Things You'll Need

- ☐ Paper
- ☐ Pen/pencil
- ☐ Computer (optional)
- ☐ Printer (optional)
- ☐ Laminating material
- ☐ Dry-erase highlighter (optional)

tip If your family is color-oriented, you can give each person a different color pen to check off, cross off, or highlight his accomplishments.

Using Laminated Checklists

Laminated checklists are another hard-copy option. You can take a master copy of your checklist and either laminate it yourself or have it laminated at your local photocopy store. Then, using dry-erase markers, you can check off or cross out each item as you do it. At the end of the day, week, or month, as the case may be, you can wipe the list clean and start all over again using the same list. A new erasable highlighter on the market can be used on a laminated list, but the amount of highlighting material to clean off will make this alternative rather messy. If you're going to write in who is responsible for each task and you're going to rotate among your family members, then remember to leave the assignment blank on the master copy and fill in the names on top of the laminate where they can be wiped off and changed.

Remember, those names will be handwritten, so if most people in your family respond better to their names if they're typewritten, then this option will not be ideal.

Things You'll Need

- ❏ Pen/pencil and 3×5-inch index cards, or Computer, Printer, and Microperforated sheets of 3×5-inch cards
- ❏ A large magnetic surface
- ❏ Small magnets
- ❏ A file card box
- ❏ File card dividers

Using 3×5 Cards

Cards are the best alternative for you if you want a hard-copy checklist where you delete the task after you've completed it. You'll put just one to do item on each card. Then you can assemble the checklist by posting all of the relevant cards. A good system for this method that won't wear out is hanging 3- by 5-inch cards with the tasks onto a large magnetic surface; the refrigerator is a traditional choice.

Of course, you can write on 3×5 index cards. If, however, you want typewriting on your cards, you can get microperforated sheets of 3×5 cards that you can print on your computer. Because the cards are reusable, you'll find that the amount of time and effort to set up the system is worth the results. As each task is completed, you can remove the card and place it back into a file box or other holder so it's available to use again the next time you create a list.

Because you'll have cards for each day of the week and cards for each month of the year, a good way to keep the cards that aren't posted currently is to use an index card file box with dividers labeled with the names of the days and months. You can make your own set using blank dividers.

Things You'll Need

❑ A desktop computer or a PDA

Using Digital Lists

A list on your desktop computer will allow you to use any method to indicate task completion. The easiest way to create a computer list that you can check off is to use the checklist option for outlines in your word processor. Or, if you don't have that option, you can simply type check marks in front of the items on your list. You can cross items out by using the strikethrough style in your word processor. You can highlight text either by using a highlight option or by changing the text color of the entry. And, of course, you can select a line of text and delete it if you want to remove the completed task.

PDA checklists will work as long as you prefer checking off or deleting completed items. In Figure 4.12, the choice has been made to check off tasks as they're finished, whereas in Figure 4.13 the choice has been made to hide the finished items. Either way, the complete list can be retrieved, so you can use it over again without having to re-create it.

FIGURE 4.12

You can easily create a checklist on a PDA.

FIGURE 4.13
You can change the settings on your PDA to do list so that you see only the items that you still have to complete.

Comparing List Types

Table 4.8 gives you a quick reference guide to see which checklist formats will work with your family's preferences.

Table 4.8   Formatting Options for Checklists

	Cross Out	Check Off	Highlight	Delete
Handwritten	Single-use paper	Single-use paper	Single-use paper	Cards
	Laminated sheet	Laminated sheet	Laminated sheet	
Typewritten hard copy	Single-use paper	Single-use paper	Single-use paper	Cards
	Laminated sheet	Laminated sheet	Laminated sheet	
Typewritten electronic	Desktop	Desktop	Desktop	Desktop
		PDA		PDA

Things You'll Need

- ❑ The time-specific lists you created earlier in this chapter
- ❑ Your family's planner

Integrating Your Checklists with Your Planner

Now you're ready to finalize your checklists and integrate them into your planner.

No matter which form of checklist your family has chosen, you should include all of the following information on each checklist:

- A description of the task
- Your time estimate for the task
- The name of the person responsible for completing the task
- A check box (only if you've chosen the check-off method)

You'll find that your monthly checklists are easier to use if you put the tasks in chronological order, as shown in Figure 4.14, because the next step is to schedule enough time each day on your planner to complete the tasks listed for that day.

FIGURE 4.14
The tasks on this monthly checklist have been arranged chronologically to make it easier to see how much time needs to be blocked off on the family planner each day.

To-Do	Day	Time est.	Who	√
buy new towels	1st Tues.	1 hr.	Mom	
clean out medicine cab.	2nd Wed.	30 min.	Mom	
wash shower curtains	3rd Mon.	30 min.	Jane	
wash master bath walls	3rd Mon.	50 min.	Dad	
wash guest bath walls	4th Mon.	40 min.	Dick	

March — bathrooms

This process gives you another opportunity to fine-tune your time-specific lists:

- If a task is listed as a daily item but doesn't happen on a particular day, then you won't schedule time for it on that day. An example would be going through the mail, which you need to do daily, except on Sundays because there's no mail delivery.

- If something seems to be missing or you notice that something is never getting done, you can use that as an indicator that you should look back and check whether you've listed it to be done at a good frequency—or whether you've listed it at all.

- If you discover that some of your time estimates are unrealistic—either too short or too long—adjust them to reflect reality. Encourage everyone to continue to try to reduce the time each task takes by becoming more efficient and proficient at it.

- Your family can decide to change the frequencies of tasks and who's assigned to do them whenever you agree that a change is appropriate.

Chapter Summary

All of the necessities of life—taking care of your family, pets, home, and money—demand a huge amount of work. In this chapter, you learned how to create comprehensive to do lists, so you can rest easy that nothing essential is falling through the cracks. And, even though everything that needs to be done seemed overwhelming at first, you learned that when you take the time to become more effective and efficient and to spread out all of the work in a reasonable schedule, you free up your mind and your time (and maybe even some money).

Before leaving this chapter, use the following checklist to make sure you haven't missed a critical step in organizing your family's schedule.

- ❏ Make a comprehensive to do list of everything you need to do to take care of the people in your family.
- ❏ Make a comprehensive to do list of everything you need to do to take care of the pets in your family.
- ❏ Make a comprehensive to do list of everything you need to do to maintain your home.
- ❏ Eliminate any tasks or parts of tasks that are really unnecessary.
- ❏ Find ways to do the remaining tasks more efficiently.
- ❏ Determine which format of checklist will work best for your family.
- ❏ Divide your large to do lists into daily, weekly, and monthly checklists.
- ❏ Give each task a time estimate.
- ❏ Assign someone to do each task.
- ❏ Block out from your schedule the time over which you have no control, such as for work and school.
- ❏ Block out enough time every day for sleep.
- ❏ Block out times on your schedule to accomplish all of the items on your checklists.
- ❏ Refine your time estimates, frequencies, and people assignments as needed.

Making sure you've scheduled life's necessities will give you the peace of mind to be able to focus on all of life's embellishments. In the next chapter, we'll begin to build those enjoyable activities into your family's schedule.

Celebrating Special Occasions

H appy lives are filled with so much more than just work and chores. Celebrations of births, anniversaries, and other important events are occasions for family and friends to get together and enjoy one another. You certainly don't want to let poor scheduling diminish the significance of the event or cause it to become a time to be endured rather than treasured. In this chapter, you'll see how to organize your family's schedule so that life's milestones can be marked by stress-free family celebrations.

In this chapter:

* Choosing, scheduling, and planning family celebrations
* Planning holidays
* Making time for important family traditions

To do list

❏ Note important dates on your family's calendar
❏ Block out time for celebrations
❏ Plan the celebrations
❏ Prepare for the events
❏ Celebrate!
❏ Take time to preserve memories of your family's celebrations

Scheduling Family Celebrations

Many excellent books and resources are available to help you plan parties and events of all kinds. However, those same books and resources frequently fail to address how you can work all of the detailed plans they suggest into your family's schedule. What we're going to look at here is how to make sure that you schedule your plans for smooth results—no all-night cleaning marathons, no last-minute runs to the gas station for bags of ice, and no short tempers.

Things You'll Need

- ❑ A calendar
- ❑ Your lists of important family dates—birthdays, anniversaries, and so on
- ❑ Your family's planner

Putting Important Dates on Your Family's Calendar

The more people you have in your family, the more things you'll have to celebrate—and the harder you'll find it to keep track of them. Making sure everybody knows what's coming up is key. So every year when you get your new planner for the next year (or at the beginning of the new year if you're using a system that doesn't require a new planner), gather the whole family together and discuss the events you already know about for the coming year. You'll have annual events such as birthdays and anniversaries, and you'll have the year's special events such as graduations and weddings.

Make sure that you enter the appropriate dates into your family's planner. You may also have some speculative possibilities. For example, you might have a good idea that the Cub Scout in your family will be receiving an award at the spring Scout dinner. These dates should get "penciled in" so that as other activities come up for the same date all family members are aware that there may be a conflict and, at most, they can make only tentative plans for that date. Throughout the year, other occasions for family celebrations will come up. The dates should be brought to everyone's attention and entered into the family planner immediately.

This initial family planning session of the year is also a good time to discuss any preliminary ideas of how you'll celebrate the important dates and who will be involved. You might want to require everyone to be available for a family dinner on each person's birthday, but mom and dad may choose to have a quiet dinner for two on their anniversary. At this point, nothing is really definite but the dates. Still, getting a feel for how each family member may be expected to participate will make the actual scheduling process easier when the time comes.

Even though all of the dates are recorded in your planner, you should safeguard against having one of those dates arrive without your having prepared for it. So, for each date you enter, also enter a note six weeks earlier reminding you that the event is upcoming.

> **caution** When it comes to important dates, don't rely on your memory; use your planner. Even the most memorable of occasions have a way of sneaking up on you. Especially, don't rely on other events to trigger your memory if those other events don't happen on a fixed date. Many national holidays are tied to such roving days as "the first Monday of the month" and can move around datewise by a whole week, so by the time they jog your memory, your special day could be a week in the past!

Setting Aside Enough Time to Celebrate

Celebrations come in all shapes and sizes, but you can categorize them into three types of activities for the purpose of working them into your family's schedule:

- Private family gatherings can produce some of the most treasured family memories. These celebrations don't involve anyone but the immediate family. They are smaller and less formal—and require less planning and preparation time. Birthday dinners (especially for the adults in the family), anniversary dinners, Mother's Day brunches, or acknowledgments of significant achievements with special desserts all fall into this category.

- Throwing full-blown parties will seem more appropriate for other events. These celebrations involve inviting people outside the immediate family. They are larger and more structured—and require more planning and preparation time. Graduation parties, weddings, and end-of-season team parties fall into this category.

- Another type of celebration is the kind where you or your family are invited guests. These celebrations can be family events hosted by extended family members or important milestones being celebrated by friends. You'll find that your planning and preparation to attend these events will be much different from the planning and preparation when you and your family are in charge.

No matter which type of celebration you're having, you'll need to be involved in four phases: planning, preparation, celebration, and memorializing.

Planning

You'll know it's time to start the planning phase when your six-week advance reminder comes up on your family's schedule. This is the time to make some crucial decisions about the flavor of the celebration. Everyone in your family who will play a part in the event should be involved in this initial phase because you want to make sure that everyone is in agreement about how the celebration will shape up.

Begin by clearly defining everyone's roles. Decide at the beginning of the planning process who will be involved in the making of key decisions about the celebration. Consider the person whose milestone you'll be celebrating and whether that person should be participating in decisions about the celebration. Children over the age of three usually have some pretty definite ideas about what type of birthday party they would like to have. On the other hand, the honoree at a retirement party might prefer to just have to show up rather than be involved in any planning.

And sometimes the party isn't really about the guest of honor at all; first-year birthday parties, infant baptism receptions, and traditional graduation dinners with grandparents tend to be more for the hosts. Of course, the planning of surprise parties by definition doesn't receive input from the person who is the reason for the party. Make especially sure to include in the planning anyone who is likely to have a strong opinion or a hesitancy to participate so she won't feel that her ideas have been overlooked.

After you've established who will be responsible for the planning of the event, you'll also want to get clear about who will make the important decisions about the celebration. You don't have to—and probably shouldn't—let one person make all of the decisions. For example, it's certainly appropriate for a six year old to be able to choose between yellow or chocolate birthday cake. At the same time, a parent, while taking into consideration the child's preference, should be the one to determine whether a party at the ice-skating rink is acceptable.

At this early point in the planning phase, you'll need a decision on what type of event it will be. You don't want to make this decision in a vacuum. Instead, use your family planner to help you, by looking to see what the weeks leading up to the event and the days immediately after the event already have in store. A logical sequence of decision-making will go as follows:

1. Decide who you'll want to attend: just your immediate family or a more extended group. One aspect of this decision is what the person who's reaching the milestone would prefer. Some people like big parties in their honor, and other people prefer quiet family gatherings. Another aspect is the type of milestone. More people invite friends to a 25th wedding anniversary celebration than to a 17th anniversary event. Sometimes the situation calls for both types of events. Many 10 year olds like to have both a family birthday dinner and a party with their friends.

2. Consider whether you want to have the event in your home or at another location. Sometimes the nature of the event will determine this answer for

you. If you're throwing an ice-skating party, then you know where it will have to be held. Other times, family circumstances lead you toward the answer. If your family budget is tight, remember that parties at home where you do most of the work are less expensive. In another case, if your general sense is that the family will be going through a very hectic time—business trips, final exams, start of soccer season, having a new roof put on the house—then going offsite may be your best choice. Sometimes it's a matter of space—the size of your house compared to the size of the guest list.

3. Decide whether the festivities will be simple or elaborate. Again, take into account the personality of the person whose accomplishment you're celebrating. If she prefers simple, then go simple; if she prefers extravagant, then go elaborate. The amount of time and money you have available also affect this decision. Generally speaking, elaborate celebrations take both more time and more money.

4. Determine whether you should opt for a labor-intensive setup or one that's easy to do. Time and money play a major role in this decision as well. If the family does all of the cleaning, cooking, and hosting, then you'll save money, but you'll need to spend the time. If you hire a cleaning service and order the food ready-made, or if you have the celebration at a restaurant, then you'll save time and energy, but you'll need to spend more money. (If you're short on both time and money, then you'll be better off if you plan more simple festivities—hamburgers at home instead of filet mignon at a fancy restaurant.) Another factor is your family members' interests. If someone in the home really enjoys making fancy individualized favors or loves cooking elaborate gourmet meals, then a labor-intensive celebration won't seem so laborious.

Table 5.1 summarizes your options for the style of your celebration. Six weeks before the event, your family should choose one of the options on each line; that's four choices in all, with the possibility of 16 different types of celebrations.

Table 5.1 Determine the Nature of the Celebration

Just family	Invited guests
At home	At another location
Simple	Elaborate
Labor intensive	Easy to do

Select one option from each row. Sixteen different combinations are possible.

Preparing

The type of celebration you choose will determine the tasks you'll need to schedule to have a successful event. By scheduling wisely and sticking to your schedule, you'll be able to enjoy the preparation process, and you'll have energy—and a pleasant attitude—left over to enjoy the party! To help you break down the preparation into its components and get them onto your family's planner, you can use the checklists and timelines in the following tables. These tables include

- Table 5.2, "If You're Attending Any Party, Either as the Host or a Guest"
- Table 5.3, "If You're Hosting the Party Somewhere Other Than Your Home"
- Table 5.4, "If You're Planning Any Party"
- Table 5.5, "If You're Having the Party in Your Home, Whether or Not You're Inviting Guests"
- Table 5.6, "If You're Inviting Guests, Whether or Not You're Having the Party at Home"
- Table 5.7, "If You're Inviting Guests to Your Home"
- Table 5.8, "If You're Planning an Elaborate Party"
- Table 5.9, "If You've Been Invited to a Party"

The way to use these tables is to select all of the ones that apply to the type of event you're planning. Then slot each of the tasks from all of those tables into your family's schedule. For example, if you were having your child's birthday party with her friends at the ice-skating rink, then you would use the timelines in Tables 5.2, 5.3, 5.4, 5.6, and 5.8. On the other hand, if you were having a birthday dinner at home with your family, then you would use the timelines in Tables 5.2, 5.4, 5.5, and 5.8. The easiest way for you to select the appropriate checklists is to read the name of each table and see whether it applies to your event; you'll use Table 5.2 for all parties, while your use of the other tables will depend on whether you're the host or the guest, whether the party will be at your home or elsewhere, and the nature of the party.

Table 5.2   If You're Attending Any Party, Either as the Host or as a Guest

4 weeks before	Decide what you'll wear.
	Try on your outfit if you already own it.
	Wash the outfit or take it to the dry cleaners, if necessary.
	Buy a new outfit, if necessary.

Table 5.2   Continued

3 weeks before	Buy the gift and card (wrapping paper, ribbon, tape). Wrap the gift. Check your cameras; buy film, batteries, videotapes, as needed. Pick up your outfit at the cleaners, if necessary.
1 day after	Take the film to have it developed.
2 days after	Pick up the photos.
3 days after	Send the photos to people who would like them.
1 week after	Put the photos in an album; create a scrapbook, if you want one.

Table 5.3   If You're Hosting the Party Somewhere Other Than Your Home

6 weeks before	Set the time, date, and location. Reserve the location for the party.
1 day before	Make sure you have enough gas in your car.

tip If you're planning a major event (such as a wedding) or any event at a popular location, inquire as soon as possible about availability, the number of months in advance you should book it, deposit requirements, and so on, to avoid being disappointed.

Table 5.4   If You're Planning Any Party

4 weeks before	Plan the menu.

Table 5.5   If You're Having the Party in Your Home, Whether or Not You're Inviting Guests

4 weeks before	Set the dates and time.
3 weeks before	Check your stock of disposable dishes and cutlery, if you're going to use disposable supplies. Buy any disposable supplies you need.
2 weeks before	Buy any nonperishable food items you'll need.
2 days before	Buy perishable food items you'll need.
1 day before	Prepare any food ahead that you can.
Day of party	Prepare any additional food you're going to serve. Order any take-out food you're going to serve.
1 day after	Clean up and put things away.

Table 5.6 If You're Inviting Guests, Whether or Not You're Having the Party at Home

4 weeks before	Buy or make invitations.
	Compile a guest list with addresses.
	Address the invitations and send them.
	Plan the party favors.
	Begin making the favors, if you're going to make them.
2 weeks before	Buy the favors, if you're going to buy them.
3 days after	Write and send thank-you notes, if appropriate.

Table 5.7 If You're Inviting Guests to Your Home

4 weeks before	Make arrangements to rent or borrow any extra chairs, tables, or tableware you'll need.
3 weeks before	Pick up anything you're borrowing.
	Clean any serving pieces that you don't use very often.
1 week before	Clean the part of the house that you won't use for the party.
4 days before	Dust and vacuum where the party will be.
2 days before	Pick up or take delivery of rental items.
	Set up the tables and chairs.
1 day before	Clean the guest lavatory.
1 day after	Return rented and borrowed items.

Table 5.8 If You're Planning an Elaborate Party

4 weeks before	Decide on a theme, if any.
	Plan the decorations.
	Begin making the decorations, if you're going to make them.
	Order the decorations, if they need to be ordered.
	Plan and hire the entertainment, if you're having any.
	Order the food, if the event will be catered.
2 weeks before	Buy the decorations, if you're going to buy them.
Day of party	Pick up any food or decorations that were special ordered.

tip When it comes time for the final preparations, you can really do yourself a favor by scheduling things so the preparations should be completed a half hour in advance of the event. That half-hour cushion leaves you time to catch your breath and begin to enjoy yourself. You'll also be prepared in case anyone arrives early. And, in the worst case, you'll have time to deal with any last-minute emergencies.

Table 5.9   If You've Been Invited to a Party

When you receive the invitation	RSVP.
	Get directions to the party.
1 day before	Make sure you have enough gas in your car.

note Does planning a party sound too overwhelming to you? Not all celebrations need to be scheduled. Very small or spur-of-the-moment celebrations can sometimes seem even more special—a glass raised in a congratulatory toast, an unexpected box of candy or bouquet of flowers, or even something as simple as a heartfelt hug!

USE YOUR SYSTEM FOR SCHEDULING CELEBRATIONS

By now, you and your family should be familiar with how to move tasks from a to do list to a schedule (see Chapter 4, "Dealing with the Necessities of Life"). You'll want to assign each task to someone who's willing and able—and, you hope, enthusiastic—to undertake it. Also continue to build on the system you've already put in place by remembering to use your weekly plan to help you decide on what days of the week to schedule each task: Writing invitations and placing orders by phone would go on your deskwork day, shopping would go on your errand day, polishing serving pieces would go on your housework day, planning decorations could go on your family day, and so on.

As you'll see, one of the first things you need to do when planning a celebration is to set the date, time, and place. You'll want to make sure when you do that you take into account conflicts—definite or anticipated—with the schedules of the people you would like to join in the celebration. If you're having a family event, you'll definitely want to use your family planner to avoid any conflicts that already exist. Then you'll want to use the planner to make a note of the event so that it will have priority over any future scheduling. If you're having a large event with many invited guests, you'll need to look at a calendar—preferably one that lists local as well as more universal happenings—and try to avoid any widespread conflicts. For example, you might decide it's prudent to avoid the day of your local school's graduation or the grand opening of a new community center.

caution Don't stockpile paper goods for parties. You can easily get drawn in on great discounts if you buy in bulk. But chances are you'll want a different style of plates and napkins the next time around. And paper goods don't keep well; they get crumpled if you don't lay them flat, and they get rippled—and too disgusting to use—if they're exposed to any moisture. When you start planning the party six weeks in advance, you'll have plenty of time to find a fresh supply of exactly what you want on sale.

R.S.V.P.?

R.S.V.P. (alternately fashioned R.s.v.p. and RSVP) is an abbreviation for the French phrase "Répondez s'il vous plaît," which means "Please respond." The corresponding English phrase is "The favour of a reply is requested." All the polite phrasing aside, from an etiquette standpoint an invitation that bears "R.S.V.P." requires a response, and the response is to be made as soon as possible. A response is required whether the invitee is accepting the invitation or sending regrets.

What does this mean to you in terms of scheduling?

❋ If you've been invited to a party, and the invitation asks for an RSVP, then you need to make up your mind fairly quickly because it is your social obligation to respond one way or the other. Some invitations indicate the date by which your reply is needed; this date is a deadline, but a quicker response is much more polite.

❋ If you're issuing invitations, then you'll want to give careful thought to whether you want to require RSVPs. Consider the following situations:

  ❋ Except with the most formal of invitations, which command a written reply, your potential guests are likely to respond by phone. These calls can result in your spending many hours catching up on news with friends and acquaintances. If your schedule is too tight to pack all of that phone time into a couple of weeks, then maybe you don't want everyone to RSVP.

  ❋ One alternative that's available to you is for you to indicate on the invitation "Regrets only." This phrase means that you want people to reply only if they won't be coming to the party. This option will provide you with some information about who may be attending, and at least the people you'll end up talking to on the phone will be different from the people you'll see at the party.

  ❋ You can save everyone—you and your guests—time and effort by not requiring any response to your invitation at all. This choice is really not as risky as it sounds. Even if you ask for a response, a certain percentage of invitees will not respond (and you'll want to make sure that you have enough of everything in case they do show up). On the other hand, even if you don't ask for a response, a certain number of people will feel the need to let you know whether or not they're coming anyway. In general, the same percentage of people show up whether or not replies were expected or received. A good "rule of thumb" is 30% to 40%, but you know your friends best, and this percentage may be different for you. The more parties you throw, the better the feel you'll have about how many people will attend.

  ❋ If you're having your party at a restaurant or party facility, you'll want a more accurate idea of who's coming so that you don't end up reserving space and paying for food that no one will use. Invitees seem to understand this and respond better in these situations.

Celebrating

After the planning and the preparation, it's finally time for the celebration itself! We're sure you don't need a lengthy explanation of what to do here. Your hard work will pay off, and you should be sure to have fun. Just a few words of caution here:

- Something is bound to not go according to plan. If you stop to think about it, probably some of your best memories—the ones that are retold over and over—are of things that went wrong; things like the dog knocking over the grill and eating all of the hamburgers. Probably the best thing you can do is be flexible and smile.

- Don't schedule anything too close after the fun. (You may have noticed in the timelines that we've even recommended leaving the cleanup until the next day.) You'll want to have some time to enjoy your accomplishment.

Preserving the Memories

We've said it before, but this point bears repeating here: The wrapping-up phase of any project is the easiest one to let slide. But next to the fun of the celebration itself, the best part of personal and family milestones is the memories—and they last a lot longer.

If someone in your family has a hobby that lends itself to memory preservation, then you're halfway there. There are many complex ways of preserving memories that some people really enjoy:

- Someone who likes video editing can take any video you have of the event and turn it into a cohesive piece that really captures the highlights.

- Digital photos, in the hands of someone with the appropriate interest, can be edited and archived, posted on the Internet, or burned onto CDs.

- Scrapbooking is an extremely popular hobby these days. Although it is time-consuming, for an enthusiast the hours spent are truly pleasant, and the result can be enjoyed for many years by many people.

note Also referred to as a memory preserver, the Snaptop case by Iris, shown in Figure 5.1, holds all of the memorabilia from an event and is designed to be stored either horizontally or vertically. Suggested retail: $5.99. Website: www.irisusainc.com

All of these hobbies take time and need to have their own place in your family's schedule (see Chapter 7, "Planning Other Fun Stuff"). In the meantime, the important step you need as you wrap up the celebration is to take enough time to set aside safely in one place all of the pieces you want preserved.

Perhaps in the past—if you set aside things at all—you've used shoeboxes or shopping bags to keep such things together. And, unfortunately, if you've ever gone back to create a more presentable remembrance, you've probably found that some of what you kept has been crunched, munched, or moisture-damaged. Now that you're becoming more organized, you'll probably want to use something a little less vulnerable. "Memory preservers" such as the one illustrated in Figure 5.1 allow you to corral everything you'll need—photos, videos, CDs, themed paper plates and napkins, a copy of the invitation, and the like—and keep it in good condition. In fact, if no one in your family has any inclination to spend time creating an artistic

note Another valuable exercise you might want to include in your wrap-up activities is to "debrief" the celebration. Have your family members talk over what they liked and didn't like and incorporate those opinions into your future event planning.

If you celebrate the same event each year, consider keeping a notebook containing your guest list, menu (including quantities), list of decorations, and any reminders or suggestions for the next time.

Time Optimizer

memory, these plastic containers may be your last step. If you label and shelve them, you'll be able to take them out and reminisce any time you want.

FIGURE 5.1

A plastic scrapbook case can be either the first or the last step in preserving your precious memories.

Planning Your Holidays

Holidays are great occasions to take a break from the normal routine, relax, and catch up with family and friends. Unfortunately, for many people whose lives are already too hectic, holidays become just another stressor to add to the list. Now that you're organizing your family's schedule, holidays can return to being the happily anticipated special days that they were when you were a child.

Choosing the Holidays You'll Celebrate

The list of holidays you can celebrate in a year is virtually endless; a quick review of a common calendar will give you at least 20 possibilities. Every religious tradition comes with its own array of both major and minor holidays. Ethnic heritages—yours or some-

one else's—provide you with more choices. You won't want to overlook national holidays either. Plus, there's a growing array of miscellaneous secular holidays as well. Some holidays have been extended to entire seasons.

Your goal, as always, will be to please the most people in the family without making anyone feel overwhelmed. Start by listing the holidays that your family has always celebrated. Don't be hesitant to make everyone take a closer look to see whether there is any holiday on this list that no one feels the need to celebrate, because sometimes everyone in the family outgrows, or needs a break from, the same holiday at the same time. Next, look to see whether there are any holidays the family would like to add to the list. Just remember to be selective because you can't have the time and energy to celebrate everything.

caution Even holidays with extended seasons need to have a beginning and an end. Unless you own an all-year Christmas store, Christmas decorations have no place in the Easter season. Allowing yourself to keep any holiday's decorations up too long, no matter how you rationalize it, takes away from the special nature of that holiday and the ones that come after it. If you find holiday decorations fading into the background and escaping your conscious thought, then use your planner to stop yourself by making sure that when you put up the decorations, you also schedule a day and time to take down the decorations.

Of course, you can make the festivities as elaborate or as simple as you would like. For an extensive holiday season, you might include indoor and outdoor decorations, handmade crafts and home-baked goodies, dinners, parties, community outreach activities, elegantly wrapped homemade and store-bought presents, and so on. At the other end of the spectrum, your commemoration of the holiday can be something as simple as serving green gelatin for dessert on St. Patrick's Day. Whatever holiday you want to observe, in whatever way, you'll find plenty of books and magazines if you're looking for new ideas.

Incorporating the Holidays into Your Family's Schedule

The challenge we need to address here is no different than all of the challenges we're looking at in this book: how to make sure that the activities you select can be incorporated into your family's schedule for the best time with the least amount of stress. And the method for doing that should be becoming familiar to you:

1. Decide what your family wants the result to be—which options will be included and which won't.

2. Stop for a reality check to make sure your plans aren't too ambitious. Modify them, if prudent.

3. Make a list of what needs to be done to achieve your planned results.

4. Break down the list into components as simple as you need to ensure that no step will be overlooked. Don't forget preparation and wrapping up.

5. Estimate times and assign people to each component to create a checklist.

6. Schedule the items from the checklist into the family schedule.

Look at Figure 5.2 to see how one family might plan its observance of Halloween. You can use the same technique for any holiday.

tip Holiday accessories—decorations, serving pieces, and the like—can take up a lot of space, not to mention time to maintain. Sometimes simplifying what you have can actually open the door for more creativity. Consider acquiring a few basics that can serve you well on multiple holidays. A good example is a plain red tablecloth. It will be just right for Christmas (maybe with green napkins), for Valentine's Day (white or pink napkins), and any national holiday (white or blue napkins). Your choices, both in terms of how often you can use the tablecloth and in terms of specific holiday decorations, are so much greater than if you opted for holiday-themed tablecloths for each occasion.

FIGURE 5.2
This activity map serves as a to do list that will be turned into a checklist and then scheduled onto the family's planner.

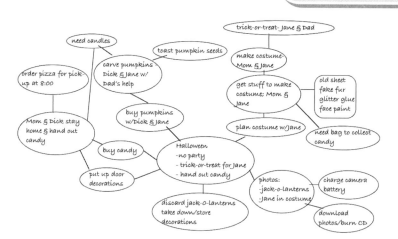

Keeping (or Losing) Family Traditions

Traditions are one of those undercurrents of life that give it a sense of timelessness and stability. With that in mind, it's only logical that traditions should evoke feelings of happiness and well-being, not feelings of difficulty and burden. So, just as you've reviewed family celebrations and holidays, you should also take a close look at your family traditions.

Do you maintain the tradition because people enjoy it or because that's what you've always done? In other words, are your family members tolerating the tradition more than they're enjoying it? The classic example that comes to mind is the holiday fruitcake, simply tolerated by so many people that it has become the subject of many jokes. Fruitcakes were at one time a grand holiday delicacy, but time has taken its toll, and, unless you have a rare fruitcake-lover in your family, this tradition is a prime candidate for retirement. Consider each of your traditions to see whether any of them is also nearing retirement age.

One way to test a tradition about which you have doubts is to suggest that it be eliminated from the festivities. Does that suggestion produce an outcry of objections? If so, then the tradition is still loved and appreciated, and your family will want to maintain it.

In some instances, you may find that the tradition is becoming burdensome, but you can't give it up because it has been entrusted to you. Are you the keeper of an heirloom that is required to be displayed or used on certain occasions? Or are you the person who has to make a certain holiday dish every year because you're the only one who has the recipe and the touch to make it like great-grandma? If you're feeling that this tradition is more like a curse—and feeling guilty about the way you're feeling, besides—now is the time to think about passing the responsibility for the tradition to someone else, just as it was once passed to you. Ask around and find someone who either loves the tradition or someone who has an avid interest in preserving family history. Then schedule a time to make that person feel special as you bestow the family trust upon him.

We've discussed keeping some traditions and ending others. Don't forget, too, that all traditions started sometime. You can begin traditions, too. When you discover an activity, big or small, that your family loves, think about making it a regular event, and it won't be long before it will become a family tradition all your own. As these recurring events become traditions, they also work to create family memories and bring your family closer together. Even teenagers who want to strike out on their own as much as possible can't resist the lure of a tradition they've loved since childhood. Whether five generations old or initiated by your immediate family, cherished traditions lend a special quality to all family celebrations.

HOW TRADITIONS CREATE MEMORIES

Our memories are made and solidified by the repetition of events that are associated with the stimulation of one or more of our senses. Certain sights, sounds, tastes, smells, and textures will always take you back to certain memories from your past. As you follow traditions with your family, so that the same sensory stimuli occur with the same activities year after year, you create powerful memories that will be treasured for generations.

Chapter Summary

In this chapter, we've detailed the mechanisms you need to put in place in your family's schedule to take most of the stress out of—and put more fun into—celebrating important events and holidays. As always, the keys are thoughtful planning, realistic expectations, and keeping everyone involved.

Before leaving this chapter, use the following checklist to make sure you haven't missed a critical step in organizing your family's schedule.

- ❏ Mark important dates on your family's calendar as soon as they are known.
- ❏ Decide what type of celebration you'll have and who will be involved in it.
- ❏ Take time to create a detailed plan for the festivities.
- ❏ Follow a timeline to take care of all preparations for the event.
- ❏ Enjoy the celebration.
- ❏ Preserve the memories through both keepsakes and traditions.

Now that you've organized the necessities in your family's life and scheduled time for major benchmarks, you should still have plenty of time left over for other activities that enhance your life. In the next chapter, we'll look at scheduling structured enrichment activities for your family.

Participating in Enrichment Activities

6

One of the things that makes life so interesting is that we each have our own unique combination of interests and talents. Participating in structured activities is an important way to discover and pursue those interests and talents. For children who have limited life experiences and for adults who have wide-ranging interests and want to try lots of new things, selecting the right mix of activities to keep you growing without turning the logistics into a stress-inducing dash from one place to the next is a real challenge.

This is the point where the scheduling skills and the effectiveness techniques you've already learned in the first five chapters of this book will have a magnified impact on your family's life. Because you've already scheduled all of the necessities of life, and you're accomplishing them efficiently, you'll be able to see easily whether various pursuits will dovetail with—or disrupt—your family's schedule. In this chapter, you'll learn how to help all of your family members make good enrichment activity choices and how to incorporate these important activities into your family's schedule. You'll learn how to manage your schedule so that everyone can participate in enrichment activities without causing scheduling conflicts.

Things You'll Need

- ❏ Brochures and/or basic information (what, when, where, and why) for all of the activities your family members are considering
- ❏ Your family's planner

To do list

- ❏ Consider the reason(s) for wanting to participate in each activity
- ❏ Rank the participants' interests in each activity
- ❏ Have the participants fill out the self-assessment questionnaires to determine whether they should try (or continue) each activity
- ❏ Schedule a reevaluation of your family's enrichment activities into your family's planner at regular intervals

Deciding How to Spend Your Time

You think your three year old should learn how to swim and attend the library story hour. Your five year old wants to play soccer on a team with his friends, not take piano lessons. Your eight year old would like to continue in Scouting, join Little League, and try out for a part in your community's summer play production. Your teenager is on the school track team, plays in the school band, and wants to take private golf lessons. You would like to continue participating in your book group and take a wine-tasting course in advance of your upcoming business trip. And your spouse wants to join you for the wine-tasting course and take a class in website design. How do you decide whether your family should try to do it all?

Analyzing Your Options

Even with all of the open time you've created in your family's schedule, you'll want to choose enrichment activities wisely. You should analyze the value of the activity in terms of the benefits it will provide in relation to its cost to your family in terms of money, time, and energy. To that end, you need to decide what the purpose of participation in the activity would be:

- Does the participant have a particular interest in the activity? Perhaps a brief exposure to the subject through school, work, reading, television, or the Internet has piqued an interest to learn more about it or to try it for oneself.
- Is the activity fun? Maybe the reason for participating is nothing more complicated than the fact that the person enjoys spending her time that way.
- Are there benefits to the activity? Some children need physical activities to expend their boundless energy or to develop their coordination; an adult might need a physical activity to improve his fitness. Still other activities may help the participant achieve a goal: A student may improve her test scores or an adult may learn how to manage her finances.
- Is it a social activity? Young children need to learn how to relate to other people; older children need to have activities in common with their friends; adults need interaction with other adults.
- Is the participant's interest in the activity purely exploratory? Some people, especially children, don't know whether they'll be interested in pursuing an activity until they give it a try. Some adults have ideas of things they've always wanted to try and finally get the opportunity.

tip Enrichment activities don't have to be individual activities. Consider parent/child classes (swimming, art, storytelling), multiple child activities (three siblings in the same ice-skating show), and family enrichment (everyone attending a tour at a local museum), all of which can actually ease your scheduling dilemmas.

In general, parents should probably expose their children to a broad range of activities, so they can develop and explore their interests, whereas the older members of the family will probably already have a pretty good idea of what they would like to do. Once a person has given a particular pursuit a try, then his degree of interest will start to develop. You can roughly gauge this degree of interest using a five-point scale.

1. Interest may be minimal. In that case, consider these options:
    - If the reason for the activity was exploratory, then there is no reason to continue the activity. The person should move on to try another activity that may prove more captivating.
    - If the reason for the activity was to be sociable, then the social benefits must be weighed against the dislike of or boredom with the activity. Perhaps other, more appealing activities afford an opportunity to socialize with the same group of people. Perhaps this group's choice of activities is an indication that this is the wrong group with which to socialize.

- If the activity offers a benefit—personal improvement, and so on—you need to determine whether a more pleasurable activity will supply the same benefit or whether the benefit is so great that the activity must be continued. Keep in mind that if the participant really dislikes the activity, the benefit may never be realized even if he continues the activity.

2. The activity may be a pleasant pastime.

   Regardless of the reason for participating, if the activity is a pleasant enough pastime, it can be continued until such point as it interferes with the pursuit of activities that are more interesting or provide greater benefits.

3. The activity may become an avocation.

   If the person develops a true interest in a pursuit, then she'll want to continue to have her life include an enrichment activity to improve her knowledge or skill in that area.

4. The activity can be the person's life's work.

   Whether a person's interest leads him to pursue a related vocation, or whether the person's vocation leads to engaging in the enrichment activity, self-improvement in the area of one's career generally carries with it a high benefit.

5. The activity may turn out to be the person's passion.

   Passions coupled with true talent are rare, but when they exist, they become real challenges to organizing the family's schedule. We're all familiar with stories from the sports and music worlds in which entire families' lives have revolved around ensuring that the talented, passionate child has been able to pursue his dream of greatness. If your family finds itself in this position, specialists are available to help you make the appropriate choices and adjustments for your family.

What you'll want to keep in mind as you work your way through incorporating enrichment activities into your family's schedule is that you should consider where along the interest scale each activity ranks for each member of the family. This evaluation will help you choose wisely among the many options available to you. The higher up the interest scale the activity rates, the more time—both the individual's and the family's—you'll want to dedicate to the activity.

THE VALUE OF PIANO LESSONS

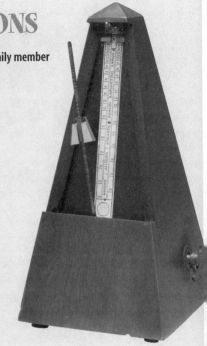

Piano lessons are a good example of an enrichment activity that you or a family member might undertake for its benefits, both obvious and hidden.

In addition to the ability to play music, the more obvious benefits include

* An improved ability to concentrate
* Greater confidence in oneself
* Improved hand-to-eye and body coordination

Some of the more hidden benefits may include

* Enhanced brain neural-circuitry for spatial-temporal reasoning
* Thicker nerve fibers between the two hemispheres of the brain
* Improved object assembly skills in preschoolers
* Higher math test scores for elementary school students
* Better verbal memory
* Higher SAT scores
* Stress relief

Sorting Out Your Preferences

The number of people in your family and their ages will affect your family's method of making choices for each person's enrichment activities. If you have only three or four people to consider, you may find that making a decision on each activity as the opportunity arises will work for your family. On the other hand, if you have more people to consider, or you have a person who wants to do everything, then you may find that establishing some ground rules first works better.

The first step is to decide whether the potential participant should consider the activity at all. The questionnaire in Table 6.1 is a tool that can help make that determination.

Table 6.1   Should You Try an Enrichment Activity?

Answer the question. Parents may answer on behalf of their child, if appropriate.	Enter the number of your answer.

a. Do you want to find out if you'll like the activity?
  1. No
  2. Yes
  3. Already know you like it	

b. Does something about it interest you?
  1. No
  2. Don't know
  3. Yes	

c. Does it sound like fun?
  1. No
  2. Yes	

d. Will participating in the activity make you a more well-rounded person (for example, add physical activity to an inactive lifestyle, expand your knowledge)?
  1. No
  2. Yes	

e. Will the activity help you attain a goal (for example, physical fitness, improved coordination, better grades, a promotion)?
  1. No
  2. Maybe
  3. Yes	

f. Do you like the people involved with it?
  1. No
  2. Don't know
  3. Yes	

Total	

Scoring:

5–7	Don't spend your time on it.
8–10	Try it if it fits easily into your schedule.
11–13	Try to work it into your schedule.
14–16	Give it priority over your other choices.

After your family is engaged in a set of activities, that doesn't mean the decision process is over. The questions of whether to continue activities and whether to try new ones need to be considered whenever it's time to sign up for the next session or season and whenever something new presents itself. Each participant should ask himself the questions found in Table 6.2 every time he's getting ready to renew his participation.

tip If your family is having a hard time remembering to assess enrichment options on a regular basis, then schedule the reevaluation process as an event in your family's planner.

Keep in mind that young children rarely have an appreciation of what their options are, so they may say they want to continue with an activity because they aren't even aware that a more appealing choice exists. Older children tend to fall into routines and may have a sense that sticking with what they're doing will be less effort than switching to something else, even if the new activity would be more fun in the end. Adults, who don't have parental pressure to deal with, frequently overlook the fact that they have any options at all and simply avoid personal enrichment altogether. These are all reasons why it's important for your family to reevaluate your members' enrichment choices at regular intervals.

Table 6.2   Should You Continue an Enrichment Activity?

Answer the question. Parents: Try to let your child answer the questions for himself.	Enter the number of your answer.
a. Does the activity interest you?	
1. No	
2. Yes	
b. Do you enjoy doing it?	
1. No	
2. Yes	
c. Is it helping you attain a goal or be a more well-rounded person?	
1. No	
2. Yes, but another activity would do the same thing.	
3. Yes, and no other activity would do the same thing.	

Table 6.2   Continued

Answer the question. Parents: Try to let your child answer the questions for himself.	Enter the number of your answer.

d. Is there another activity you would rather do or try?
    1. Yes
    2. No	

e. Do you like the people involved with it?
    1. No
    2. Yes, but I do lots of other things with them, too.
    3. Yes, and this is one of the few things I do with them.	

Total	

Scoring:

5–6	Don't sign up for it again.
7–9	Sign up again if it fits into your schedule.
10–12	Sign up for it again if at all possible.

Avoiding Scheduling Conflicts

Of course, determining which pursuits benefit and appeal to each family member is only half of the process. The important issue of working the activities into your family's schedule remains.

You cannot be in two places at the same time. By ignoring or denying this basic fact, many families create a great deal of tension and stress. Now that you're taking control and organizing your family's schedule, you'll be able to deal with scheduling conflicts before they happen and avoid all of the resulting unpleasantness.

caution Just because someone is good at something doesn't mean it's the right choice as one of that person's enrichment activities.

DON'T PLAN TO BE LATE

Planning to arrive at an event late is a way of avoiding the responsibility of making a hard choice in the first place. Being late carries with it lots of disadvantages:

* It's impolite. It interrupts the proceedings and shows a disregard for the people who made the effort to get there on time.

* It's a bad habit. It connotes an uncaring attitude toward your personal performance.

* It's stressful. Even if you think you're okay with arriving late, your level of stress is probably higher than if you were on time.

* It reduces the respect you receive. People figure if you don't care about your schedule and time, then they shouldn't have to care either.

* It reduces your success. Athletes late to team practices and students late to class don't perform as well as those who arrive on time.

If you take the time to plan ahead, you'll find that you have plenty of options to arrange your time so that you're late only in the rare instance when circumstances beyond your control are involved. If you really stop to think about the situation, making the effort to organize your family's schedule is pointless if, in the end, you still plan to live in a frazzled way.

To do list

- ☐ Eliminate activities with overlapping time frames
- ☐ Schedule time for drivers and spectators, as well as participants
- ☐ Resolve conflicts before they happen

Choosing Between Overlapping Activities

Unfortunately, for all but the dullest of people, there will always be more enticing options than there is time available. So, you can at least begin whittling down the choices by accepting the fact that you can't participate in two activities that take place at the same time. This rule applies to schedules that overlap as well. Your rewards for making a tough choice up front will be greater focus and less stress later.

If one activity meets on Mondays and Wednesdays, and the second activity meets on Wednesdays and Thursdays, then you need to recognize that the two of them are mutually exclusive. Rationalizing that you can skip each activity just once every other week will result in your receiving less than half the benefit of either activity. Plus, you'll constantly be faced with the almost paralyzing dilemma of which one to attend on each Wednesday.

In addition, don't forget to include travel time when determining what activities your schedule can accommodate. Two activities that run back-to-back but are in locations 30 minutes apart still require you to be in two places at the same time; you'll be traveling between the activities when you should already be at the second activity.

Scheduling Drivers, Spectators, and Other Family Participants

Make sure that you take into account everyone whose time will be involved. Hidden scheduling conflicts can exist when someone else is needed in addition to the primary participant. Especially for young children, you must remember that it's not just their time that you have to consider, because someone has to chauffeur them to and from the activity. If you have only one person in the family who can drive, then you can't let one child have sports practice on one side of town at the same time your other young child has an art class on the other side of town.

The only way around having to make a choice between the two activities is to arrange for someone else to drive one of the children, and, to keep things running smoothly, you need to do that before you sign up for both activities. You'll also want to look into carpooling options if one child's activity will require that your other children accompany you on a long drive to and from the activity because that's not a good use of their time, either.

Some activities require family involvement by their nature. Events that have an audience or spectators—music recitals, sports competitions, and so on—really need family members present to support the participant. When making the choice to become involved in these pursuits, make sure that family members have room in their schedules. If, for some reason, family support isn't possible, this information should be disclosed to the participant before signing up for the activity.

Resolving Conflicts with Other Family Events and Activities

Next, look at what already exists on your family's schedule. If the summer league playoffs for a particular sports activity will take place during the week that your family has scheduled its annual vacation, then you'll need to make some adjustments up front. Is summer league a really high priority item? Or would another activity be equally satisfying and not create a conflict? Are the dates for the family vacation unchangeable because there's no other time you can take off from work or you've made a nonrefundable deposit? Or can you shift the vacation to another week without causing any new conflict?

If adjustments can be made to accommodate everyone, then that's great. If not, then the family will have to settle on a hard decision. The most important point is that you make the decision before signing up for the activity, so the conflict is dealt with before it becomes a reality.

THE BEST USE OF YOUR TIME IN THE CAR

You've probably figured out that the more children you have who aren't old enough to drive and the more activities those children undertake, then the more time the adults in the family will spend in the car driving those children where they need to go. And, because having a smooth-running family schedule depends, in part, on making the best use of your time, it makes sense for us to take a few minutes to discuss productive ways for you to use the time you'll be spending in your car.

If you find yourself sitting in the car waiting for your kids to come out of locker rooms or lessons:

* You might find you have enough time to pay your bills or catch up on your correspondence. We discussed how to set up a portable home office back in Chapter 4, "Dealing with the Necessities of Life."

* You have plenty of work to do right in the car. The dashboard and the inside of the windows frequently need dusting or cleaning. If you keep a package of premoistened wipes in your glove compartment, you can use a few spare moments to spiff up your car's interior. If you keep a small plastic bag handy—either recycled from shopping or a zip-closure bag—you can de-clutter your glove box and gather and seal up the trash from around the inside of your car. Younger children really enjoy helping with these tasks, so you can keep them from becoming bored and restless by letting them help. Or let them do the cleanup on their own while you pay the bills.

You can even use the time you're on the road productively:

* You can absorb a lot of information about what's going on in the world by keeping your radio tuned to a National Public Radio station. Your kids will learn some current events, too. You may find that you no longer have to watch news on TV, which is largely teasers and commercials and can waste a lot of your time. You may be able to cut down on your newspaper and news magazine time (and expenses), too.

* Your car is one of the few places where you can have a totally private conversation with the other people you're with. You can take this opportunity to have some real heart-to-heart conversations with your captive audience. Just be careful not to get involved in emotional discussions that may distract the driver too much and lead to unsafe driving.

* If you're transporting both your children and some of their friends, take the chance to listen to some of their conversations. You may find you can pick up a lot more information about what's going on in their lives at school than you can by asking them directly and receiving the legendary "nothing" answer.

Please be aware that you'll miss out on a lot of these benefits if you rely heavily on cell phones and DVDs to keep your children occupied.

And always remember to put safety and health first. This means the driver should *not*

* Talk on a handheld cell phone. More and more municipalities are making this dangerous activity illegal. If the driver also has children in the car, talking on the phone may well be one distraction too many.

* Finish her personal grooming. People who comb their hair, polish their nails, or apply makeup while driving can't have their hands or attention where they need to be in order to drive safely.

* Eat. Not only is eating while driving a distraction, it's bad for digestion. If you don't have time to stop for 15 minutes to eat, then you've packed your schedule too tightly.

As your family continues to work toward an ever more organized schedule, consider following these steps whenever potential scheduling conflicts come up:

1. Make sure all known events are listed in the family planner (for example, birthday celebrations, sports competitions, piano recitals, business trips).

2. Remember that events posted in the planner always have priority over unposted events if a solution or compromise can't be reached.

3. Discuss a potential conflict as soon as it arises.

4. Look for a way to eliminate the conflict.

5. Practice good negotiating skills if the conflict can't be eliminated and look for a solution that will provide a win-win situation for everyone. (Example: In exchange for moving your daughter's party to a day other than her birthday so the family can attend her brother's tuba recital, you'll allow her to let her two best friends sleep over on her birthday.)

6. Be aware of—and resigned to—the need for compromise if you cannot find a win-win situation for everyone involved. In other words, don't create the conflict and figure you'll resolve it later. (Example: Because your son's track meet is at the same time as your daughter's piano recital, they know well in advance that they have to settle for the fact that their father will attend the recital and their mother will attend the track meet.)

FAMILY MEETINGS

You'll have noticed that selecting enrichment activities for each member of your family needs a lot of coordination—and sometimes negotiation—among everyone in the family. Sometimes this coordination requires the family to get together to discuss the plans. And sometimes, to convey the importance of the discussion, someone in the family—usually one of the parents—calls for a family meeting.

Finding a time in the family's schedule to hold a meeting can be a scheduling problem all its own. So, your best bet may be to plan to have the meeting whenever you can get the whole family assembled—and you can get creative in finding that occasion:

❊ When your family eats dinner together—which you may find you're more able to do the more you organize and coordinate your family's schedule

❊ If you offer to take everyone out for ice cream

❊ In the car on the way to a baseball game

Don't try to have a meeting when people may be hungry, sluggish, or in a hurry to go somewhere else.

Before you get everyone together, make sure that you're prepared with the information you need to resolve your scheduling issues. Maybe you'll need to have other family members get information and thoughts together in advance as well.

In the business world, there is an ever-growing recognition that companies should hold as few meetings with as few people as possible. You would be wise to adopt this same philosophy at home. The occasional meeting that really accomplishes something will hold everyone's interest. A meeting held on a weekly or monthly basis, whether needed or not, will quickly have family members giving little priority to attending or paying attention. Call for a meeting only if there is truly a need for an exchange of ideas with discussion. And involve only the people in your family who can contribute important questions, ideas, and solutions related to the meeting's purpose. For example, your eight year old doesn't need to attend a meeting to decide who will drive your five year old to ballet class, and your teenager doesn't need to attend a meeting to decide whether your eight year old should play soccer or baseball.

Always aim for effective family meetings that produce exciting ideas and solutions.

To do list

- ❏ Create a to do list for each activity
- ❏ Estimate the amount of time each item will take
- ❏ Decide who needs to be involved in each task
- ❏ Schedule each item into the participant's personal schedule and the family's planner
- ❏ Store each activity's equipment in a portable container
- ❏ Check periodically to make sure your family hasn't signed up for more activities than it can handle

Applying the Basics

Selecting your family's mix of enrichment activities is an ongoing process, but as each decision to participate is made, you, of course, must complete the process of incorporating the activity into your family's planner. Without this blueprint, you'll quickly find your family being unprepared and missing events. And, as you're fully aware by now, with the getting-ready and wrapping-up phases, there's more to scheduling the activity than just writing the meeting time on your calendar.

Scheduling All Phases of the Activity

The decision to take music lessons, for example, will entail all of the items listed in Table 6.3. Participating in a sport will require time in the schedule for all of the steps in Table 6.4. Participating in Scouts will involve setting aside both fixed times and flexible times to meet all of the requirements and enjoy all of the rewards, as you can see from Table 6.5.

note Whatever your activities, by now you should know that you need to create a comprehensive to do list, break it down into as many small components as you need, estimate the amount of time each item will take, indicate who needs to be involved in each task, and then schedule each item into the participant's personal schedule and into the family's planner.

Table 6.3   Music Lessons To Do List

Purchase music books or sheet music.

Rent or buy instrument.

Rent or buy instrument case.

Tune the instrument.

Repair the instrument.

Buy spare parts for the instrument, if appropriate.

Clean the instrument.

Practice.

Attend lessons.

Invite family/friends to recital or performance.

Attend recital or performance.

Table 6.4   Sports To Do List

Purchase or rent equipment.

Maintain/clean equipment.

Engage in physical conditioning.

Practice.

Participate in games/competitions.

Invite family/friends to games/competitions.

Attend parties after games/competitions.

Travel.

Table 6.5 Scouting To Do List

Attend regular meetings.

Work on projects.

Earn merit badges.

Buy uniform.

Clean uniform.

Sew badges on uniform.

Buy/borrow camping equipment.

Pack for camping.

Go camping.

Clean camping equipment.

Attend award banquets.

March in parades.

Participate in community service projects.

Setting Up Systems to Save Time

With activities that demand so much involvement by so many people in your family, you'll be much better able to maintain a steady pace if you set up some systems to handle the routine aspects of the activities as efficiently as possible.

All structured enrichment pursuits require the participants to attend practices, lessons, performances, events, or classes. And they all require the participants to bring with them some amount of equipment or supplies. An easy way to cut down on lost minutes and stress is to make sure that each activity's stuff is stored in a portable container. Tote bags or duffle bags work well for lots of different types of equipment and are easy to fill, store, and grab.

If you're dealing with more delicate music or sports equipment, you might find it worth investing in a pack especially designed for the particular instrument (see Figure 6.1) or sport (see Figure 6.2). These packs are designed for easy carrying, and many of them are available as backpacks for hands-free and back-friendly portability. They're also designed to contain all of the accessories that go along with

note Musical instrument cases are available for almost any instrument. You can find a variety of options for your instrument on the Internet by using your favorite browser and a search phrase consisting of the name of your instrument and the word "case" (example: cello case). One company that makes cases for a wide assortment of instruments is PRO TEC International. Suggested retail: $35–$179. Website: www.ptcases.com

the main equipment. If you have a Scout in your family, consider supplying him with a hand-powered flashlight for camping to eliminate the need for last-minute scrambling to replace weak or dead batteries (see Figure 6.3).

FIGURE 6.1

A musical instrument case that has compartments for music, accessories, and spare parts will keep everything the family musician needs together and protected from damage.

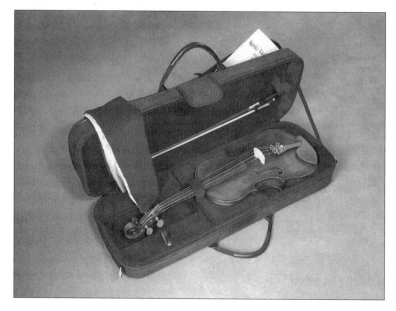

FIGURE 6.2

Specialized sports bags provide compartments for uniquely shaped equipment.

note Sports equipment bags are available for almost any sport. You can find a variety of options for your sport on the Internet by using your favorite browser and a search phrase consisting of the name of your sport and the words "equipment bag" (example: hockey equipment bag). One company that makes equipment bags for a wide variety of sports is Wilson Sporting Goods. Suggested retail: $15–$110. Website: www.wilson.com

Product Note

FIGURE 6.3

The user generates the electricity to operate this flashlight by squeezing its handle, so it never needs batteries.

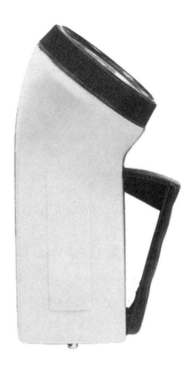

note Coghlan's Dynalite flashlight works using friction instead of batteries. Suggested retail: $6.59. Website: www.coghlans.com

Product Note

Periodically Reevaluating Enrichment Activity Schedules

If you find that your family—or a member of your family—is having trouble keeping up with every commitment, then you shouldn't hesitate to insist upon a reevaluation of your situation. Although many choices will be appealing, there's no need to try to do everything at once. You can encourage—or require—family members to limit themselves to a certain small number of activities at a time. Then, when it's time to reregister for the activity, find out whether they would like to stick with it or give something new a try. The real advantages to enrichment activities are that they don't require a long-term commitment and that participants can move in and out of them with relative ease.

tip Remember that six or eight weeks of an activity for children will seem like a very long time because it's a large percentage of their lifetime. So, unless they have truly found their passions, switching activities at that interval will not seem too soon.

Remember that your family members need to find these pursuits enjoyable, not stress-inducing, for them to be beneficial. There are many factors to consider when selecting the right blend of activities for each person, but how those activities fit the individual's and the family's schedule is one very important determinant.

Chapter Summary

In this chapter, you learned how you can build some significant personal improvement endeavors for each family member on top of your smooth-running base. You saw how you can do this without disrupting the flow of your family's schedule so that you can maximize the benefit from these activities by participating in them without adding tension. You saw that a crucial component of your success is understanding how one individual's activities affect the entire family's schedule and how you must reflect that ripple in your family's planner system.

Before leaving this chapter, use the following checklist to make sure you haven't missed a critical step in organizing your family's schedule.

- ❑ Learn each family member's enrichment activity options.
- ❑ Evaluate and rank those options.
- ❑ Consider the options in light of the family's other plans.
- ❑ Choose the family's current enrichment activities.
- ❑ Schedule all aspects of the activities into your family's planner.
- ❑ Reevaluate your selections at regular intervals.

Next, we'll look at completing your family's schedule by adding in some other fun pastimes, which are really the reward of a well-planned and organized family schedule.

Planning Other Fun Stuff

7

L ife is about more than totally structured activities. Some people—perhaps even you—worry that if they organize their entire schedule, they'll lose their spontaneity and creativity. Instead, what really happens is that you orderly and efficiently accomplish everything that you have to get done, and you end up with extra time that's yours to use as you would like.

Think how much easier it is to enjoy a glass of iced tea with a friend when you aren't thinking about piles of laundry and how you're going to tell your five year old that you can't attend her piano recital because you scheduled an important business meeting at the same time. On the other hand, you don't want your carefully won free time to dissipate without enjoying it, so you'll need to do a little planning and scheduling of your leisure time, too. In this chapter, you'll learn how to make the most of your leisure time. This chapter focuses on scheduling considerations when planning family vacations, enjoying the time that you're gone, and getting through the "re-entry" period gracefully and easily. You'll also learn about securing time in your schedule for hobbies, socializing with friends, and just relaxing—with nowhere you have to be and nothing you have to do.

In this chapter:

* Planning family vacations
* Finding time to enjoy your hobbies
* Getting together with friends
* Enjoying your free time

To do list

- ❏ Use the timetable in Table 7.1 to prepare for your vacation
- ❏ Create an itinerary that will satisfy all your family members and keep them cheerful
- ❏ Use the timetable in Table 7.2 to schedule wrap-up tasks for the week after your vacation
- ❏ Have fun!

Family Vacations

Some of the best family memories come from family vacations, when everyone put aside the routine tasks and "got away from it all." And although some of us will feel nostalgic when we recall all-night packing sessions and mad scrambles to get a hotel room when the destination town was booked solid for a motorcycle rally, the stress caused by these incidents at the time may well make us think that some planning ahead would have been a better idea.

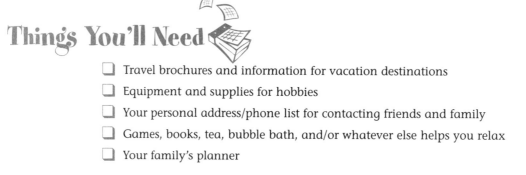

Things You'll Need

- ❏ Travel brochures and information for vacation destinations
- ❏ Equipment and supplies for hobbies
- ❏ Your personal address/phone list for contacting friends and family
- ❏ Games, books, tea, bubble bath, and/or whatever else helps you relax
- ❏ Your family's planner

Before You Go

From a scheduling standpoint, the most important thing to do when you're planning a family vacation is to make sure that everyone's calendar is clear so that everyone can go on the vacation. You'll want to plan far enough in advance that everyone actually has a block of open days on the planner, but you don't want to plan so far in advance that lots of unforeseen conflicts are likely to arise. If a few adjustments and compromises need to be made to individuals' schedules, the sooner you can make them, the better. After you've settled on the dates, you should immediately block them off on your family's planner so no one will make the mistake of scheduling something else for the same time.

Deciding What Vacation You'll Take

The next step is to make some key decisions about the nature of your vacation so that you know what else you need to prepare and schedule.

Some people like to plan a vacation almost as much as they like to go on one. Other people find the planning a chore and prefer to have someone else do it for them. Early in your preparations, you'll need to decide if you want to

- Work through a travel agent
- Book everything yourself via the Internet
- Do it yourself by telephone

Your choice will impact your schedule because travel agents are available only certain hours, the Internet is open 24 hours a day, and the times you can phone depend on the time zone of your destination.

Then you need to decide what kind of vacation you would like to take. Different families prefer different types of accommodations:

- Camping
- Being house guests of family or friends
- Renting a condominium
- Staying at a hotel, motel, inn, or bed & breakfast
- Cruising on a ship

Your preference will factor into when you'll need to make the arrangements and what you'll need to take with you.

There are also different styles of vacations:

- Tours on which all of your transportation, accommodations, meals, and sightseeing are predetermined
- Highly planned vacations for which you've decided where you'll stay and what you'll do every day

> **tip** If you need to have any maintenance work done on your car before your trip, then make sure you have it done at least a week in advance of your departure. That way, if the mechanic doesn't get something put back just right, you'll have time to discover the problem and get it fixed before you have the whole family in the car and are on the road.

- Loosely planned vacations for which you've booked your accommodations for each night but haven't decided how you'll spend your time each day

- Free-form vacations for which you have a general idea of where you're headed, but exactly where you'll end up and what you'll do on any given day isn't arranged

- Vacations on which you plan to do a lot of sightseeing

- Vacations on which you plan primarily to recreate and relax

The style you select for each trip you're planning will make a difference in the amount of preparation you need to do before your travels and the amount of time you'll need to structure during your travels.

Scheduling Vacation Preparations

After you've settled on the nature of your get-away, you'll want to begin scheduling the preparations into your family's planner. If a step is needed, Table 7.1 will give you an idea of when to schedule it. Planning a vacation should really be a project that involves the entire family, so you'll notice that this is one of the rare instances in which several family meetings will be a good idea. You'll also notice that you should plan ahead for the first couple of days after your vacation (see Table 7.2 later in the chapter) so that you can settle back into your routine without having to strain your brain.

caution Explain to everyone in the family that you shouldn't discuss when you'll be away anywhere that people you don't know and trust may hear you. Especially keep this point in mind in circumstances such as when you're asking the post office to hold your mail; perhaps making the request by phone, rather than in person, would be a good idea. You don't want to ruin your vacation by returning to a burglarized house.

Table 7.1 Timetable for Vacation Preparation

8 weeks to 12 months before	Set budget.
	Select destination (family meeting #1).
	Decide on the type of accommodations.
	Decide on mode(s) of travel.
	Book accommodations.
	Apply for or renew passports, if necessary.
8 weeks before	Get tour books and brochures.
7 weeks before	Discuss sightseeing ideas (family meeting #2).
6 weeks before	Continue learning about your destination.

Table 7.1 Continued

4 weeks to 12 months before	Book travel or get car tune-up.
4 weeks before	Make arrangements for your pets. Finalize your travel wardrobe. Prepare a packing list for everyone.
3 weeks before	Finalize your itinerary (family meeting #3). (If you're mapping out your itinerary in detail, make sure you double-check the opening and closing times of attractions first.) Make sure you have the right luggage.
1 week before	Arrange for house sitting (mail delivery, newspaper delivery, watering plants, caring for lawn, and so on). Arrange transportation to the airport, if necessary. Make sure you have an adequate supply of prescription medications, if applicable. Schedule items from the post-vacation timetable (Table 7.2) into your planner.
2 days before	Do laundry.
1 day before	Pack. Set light timers.
The day you leave	Adjust thermostat. Lock all windows and doors.

PACKING LISTS

If you don't plan your packing properly, you can end up being frustrated at two extremes: Either you'll not know what to take and, in a last-minute frenzy, pack way too much, or you'll forget something and then have to do without it or spend your precious vacation time and money shopping for it.

Developing a thorough packing list for each family member will eliminate these problems. Having a master list saved on your computer will keep you from having to reinvent the wheel each time someone in your family travels. Start by listing every possible thing you might want to take on every possible type of vacation (and business trip, too). You should list some items—such as clothing, toiletries, and reading material—separately for each person. You can list other items that are more communal—such as maps, snacks, and first aid supplies—just once.

Along the same line as the grocery lists we discussed in Chapter 4, "Dealing with the Necessities of Life," you can either print off a copy of the entire list and then check off what you'll need for the specific trip at hand, or you can modify the document on your computer for each trip and print the customized list containing only what you need to pack each time. Some people even like to pack the list and take it with them; they can then use it as a repacking list to make sure nothing is left behind when they head home.

While You're There

Whether you've chosen a highly structured itinerary or a more free-form adventure, scheduling your family's time while you're actually on vacation should be much easier than scheduling it when you're at home. One reason is that your regular maintenance items are not in play. Also, because you'll be away from many of the things that normally distract you, you'll have fewer options and can focus more on the activities at hand. No matter what type of vacation you're on, you're bound to be able to enjoy a less-structured schedule.

Keep in mind the following two key elements for a good time:

- Make sure to include something for everyone. Especially if you have children in a wide age range or with very different interests, be careful to assure that no one feels her preferences are being ignored. Sometimes it's even fun to split up during the day and get together and recount the day's adventures over dinner.

- Make sure that everyone has enough rest and sleep. (See Chapter 4.) Being tired can lead to crabbiness and accidents, either of which can quickly ruin a vacation.

> **caution** If you haven't booked overnight accommodations in advance, make sure you leave time in your daily schedules for securing a place to stay.

Then have fun!

Upon Your Return

If you take the time to properly end and wrap up your vacation, you'll enjoy the rejuvenating benefits of the experience into the future. To do that, you may want to consider resisting the urge to squeeze every last minute out of your vacation; instead, you may want to return home a day earlier than you have to go back to work—or at least a few hours before bedtime.

You should also make sure before you leave on vacation that your calendar for the day after your return is free from meetings, other obligations, and deadlines. (It goes without saying that if you've been managing your schedule properly, you won't have been doing any work while on your vacation!) Table 7.2 lists some common follow-up items for you to schedule into the first few days after your return.

> **tip** If you're not going to make the effort to memorialize your trip in albums and scrapbooks, put all of the memorabilia together in a container such as the scrapbook case you read about in the section titled "Preserving the Memories" in Chapter 5, "Celebrating Special Occasions."

Table 7.2   Timetable upon Your Return from Vacation

1 day after	Go through the mail.
	Unpack completely.
	Do the laundry.
	Pick up pets, if they've been away from home.
	Take film/digital photos to be printed.
	Add any items that you forgot to take with you to your master packing list for future use.
2 days after	Put away the suitcases.
	Go grocery shopping.
	Pick up the photos.
7 days after	Edit video of your vacation, put photos in albums, create a scrapbook.
	OR
	Put all these items together in a scrapbook case.
	Find a place to keep all of your souvenirs.

Hobbies

Hobbies, activities we enjoy and can get absorbed in for hours at a time, can really help us to be more interesting and pleasant people. They can be something as neat and confined as doing crossword puzzles or as messy and far flung as playing paintball. Their common thread is that they relax us and take our minds off our cares and responsibilities.

Whatever your family members' hobbies may be, there have surely been volumes written about them. Our purpose here is not to tell you what you need to do or how to do it, but to make sure that you organize your family's schedule so you set aside time for all family members to enjoy their hobbies. As your family goes about creating and maintaining its schedule, everyone must be aware of everyone else's hobbies so that time can be allocated to their pursuit, instead of taking up each individual's apparent free time with chores such as carpooling.

Each person must also make good use of his own time so that he's prepared to engage in his hobby by having the proper equipment and supplies ready. Part of that effort involves taking care of the equipment, cleaning up, and putting it away after each hobby session.

tip Schedule life's necessities (Chapter 4) so they don't interfere with seasonally sensitive hobbies.

Socializing

Social interaction is one of the basic human needs we alluded to in Chapter 4. And as you make your family's schedule more organized, you'll find that your family will have more time for socializing.

Some social activities are planned. How much social interaction each person in your family wants to schedule separate and apart from everything else will be determined, at least to some extent, by the person's other activities. If a person's work, enrichment activities, and hobbies all involve doing things with other people, then it's possible that the person's interest in spending even more time with other people may be small. On the other hand, if the rest of a person's life doesn't afford much human contact, then some planned social activities would be a good use of that person's leisure time. The important point here is that your family members should make conscious decisions about how much social activity they need and want to work into their schedules, and their leisure time should be allocated accordingly.

At other times, socializing can be purely spontaneous. And, while the fact it's spontaneous means that, by definition, it's unplanned, that doesn't mean you can't plan your schedule to afford you more opportunities for spontaneous social encounters. For example, if you stop to get a cup of coffee at the beginning of a long day of

> **tip** Setting a date with good friends can be just the motivation you need to purge your schedule of unimportant items.

errands and run into a friend at the coffee shop, you'll be more likely to just say hello and get on with your chores. If, on the other hand, you leave the coffee for the end of the day, you might find that your errands didn't take as long as you had planned; therefore, when you run into a friend, you know that you have time to sit down and catch up on his news. The flexibility to be spontaneous is one of the great hidden benefits of an organized agenda!

Free Time

As difficult as it may be to believe, if you've chosen wisely, scheduled properly, and acted efficiently, then you'll have some totally free time left over. And, because energy and creativity are often the result of a few moments of peace, free time can be an important part of your family's schedule (see Figure 7.1).

FIGURE 7.1

To ensure that you can enjoy your hobbies, social activities, and free time, schedule them into your family's planner.

TIME	SUNDAY		FRIDAY	SATURDAY
8:00				Dad/Jane golf
9:00				
10:00				
11:00				
NOON	Mom - off-duty			
1:00	leisure time			
2:00				
3:00				
4:00	Dick - Xword			
5:00	puzzle time			
6:00			cook out &	
7:00			games with	Dick - movie w/friends
8:00			neighbors	Mom/Dad - out to dinner
9:00				
10:00				Jane - sleepover at
11:00				Mary's

No adult ever likes to hear a child say "I'm bored," nor does he like to say to himself "I don't know why I never have time to do the things I'd like to do." So, just as you need to plan ahead for the opportunity to socialize spontaneously, so, too, you must plan ahead for using free time to improve the quality of your family's life. It's no good if you or your children find you have the time to read, watch a movie, play a game, or surf the Internet if you don't have reading materials, movies, games, or a list of websites you want to visit. So, be aware of how you might like to spend your free time and keep what you'll need at hand.

Of course, the fundamental idea behind free time is that you get to use it however you want, but here are some ideas to get you thinking about it:

- Do something that makes you laugh. Laughter puts you in a happy mood, and it also boosts your immune system.
- Get some fresh air. Getting outside is good for both your mind and body, and just 10 to 15 minutes of sunshine a day allows your body to produce all of the Vitamin D it needs.
- Pamper yourself. Whether you choose something as simple as a bubble bath or as elaborate as a day at a spa, your attitude is sure to be lifted.

- Take a nap. Extra rest is always a good idea, especially if you're sleep-deprived (although we hope you've eliminated that situation by now). Enough sleep can boost both your immunity so you'll be healthier and your metabolism so you'll burn more calories.

- Daydream. Letting your mind wander can produce some amazingly creative ideas.

- Do something totally spontaneous. It can be something small like catching fireflies or something more involved like going to a movie. Then take the time to appreciate how uplifting it is that your life affords you this freedom!

Because free time provides so many benefits, each family member, as well as the master schedule-keeper, must be careful to protect each person's hard-won free time. Be careful that you don't see other people's open time as an opportunity for you to have them do something you want them to do. And, on the other hand, hold your own free time in the highest regard; you'll do your own work and chores more efficiently if you stop thinking of your leisure time as bonus time for you to do your work. If you see anyone's free time getting eroded this way, write it into your family's planner and make it an item of the highest priority.

Chapter Summary

This chapter concludes the part of this book that deals with incorporating all of your life's activities, both mandatory and discretionary, into your planning and scheduling system. You should now be able to coordinate more relaxing family vacations by having everyone participate in a thorough preparation for the getaway and a smooth re-entry into the routines of daily life. You should also be able to ensure that all family members will have time to pursue hobbies without feeling pressure to be doing something else. And they should find that they have more leisure time for socializing and some free time left over for spontaneous fun.

Before leaving this chapter, use the following checklists to make sure you haven't missed a critical step in organizing your family's schedule.

If you're planning a family vacation

- ☐ Set the dates for the vacation and clear everyone's calendars.
- ☐ Decide how you'll plan the vacation.
- ☐ Choose what type of accommodations you'll stay in.
- ☐ Determine what style of vacation you'll take.

❑ Create a vacation preparation checklist and schedule the preparatory tasks into your planner.

❑ Make sure that you plan some activities that appeal to everyone and that you've allowed enough time in the itinerary for everyone to get an adequate amount of sleep.

❑ After you return, make sure that all of your vacation memorabilia gets stored together.

If you're engaging in a hobby

❑ Make sure you have all of the supplies and equipment you need.

❑ Schedule large blocks of time for your hobby so that you can really get absorbed in it.

❑ Take the time to clean up when you're through with your hobby for the day.

❑ Respect the time that other family members have set aside to engage in their hobbies.

If you want to socialize more

❑ Plan get-togethers with friends and family.

❑ Keep your schedule loose enough to take advantage of spontaneous social encounters.

If you want to enjoy and benefit from your free time

❑ Have an idea of what you want to do during periods of free time and be prepared to do it.

❑ Don't let chores and work drag out so they encroach on what should be free time.

❑ Don't expect other family members to give up their free time to do more than their fair share of the work.

In the next part of this book, we'll look at some of the special considerations that affect family members in different age brackets and under different circumstances. By understanding each group's unique characteristics, you'll be able to fine-tune your scheduling system so that everyone becomes a happy contributor toward keeping the family's schedule running smoothly.

Part III

Scheduling for All of Your Family Members

Managing the Preschool Years

8

ny adult who has been responsible for the care of an infant has come to realize that the adult's time and activities are inextricably connected to those of the child. By the time the child reaches preschool age—roughly ages three to five—the child's schedule can begin to seem more complex than the adult's. Even though there is much written about the merits of preschool, the à la carte options of preschool activities continue to grow at a dizzying rate: story hours, nature activities, art classes, music lessons, craft classes, foreign language programs, computer training, and a host of sports activities including soccer, t-ball, tennis, golf, ice skating, and gymnastics. Is it any wonder our family schedules seem out of control?

As a parent, you should take the time for some deliberate planning to prevent both your child's and your stress levels from rising beyond the comfortable range. That's what you'll learn how to do in this chapter. This process won't take much of your time or effort, but it will make a big difference in how you feel throughout the day.

Things You'll Need

☐ Your family's planner
☐ Information about day care and preschool options

Weighing Activity Options for Preschoolers

Back in Chapter 6, "Participating in Enrichment Activities," we discussed ways to select the structured activities in which each member of your family will participate. The same process you worked through in that chapter will help you sort through the options for your preschooler. For your convenience, we'll repeat the questionnaire you filled out in Chapter 6 (with some minor modifications) in Table 8.1.

Table 8.1   Should You Involve Your Preschooler in an Enrichment Activity?

Answer the question on behalf of your child.	Enter the number of your answer.
a. Do you want to find out if your preschooler will like the activity? 1. No 2. Yes 3. Already know your child will like it	
b. Does something about it interest your child? 1. No 2. Don't know 3. Yes	
c. Does it sound like fun? 1. No 2. Yes	
d. Will participating in the activity make your child a more well-rounded person (for example, add physical activity to an inactive lifestyle, expand the child's knowledge)? 1. No 2. Yes	

Table 8.1   Continued

Answer the question on behalf of your child.	Enter the number of your answer.
e. Will the activity help your child attain a goal (for example, physical fitness, improved coordination)? 1. No 2. Maybe 3. Yes	
f. Do you and your child like the people involved with the activity? 1. No 2. Don't know 3. Yes	
Total	

Scoring:

5–7	Don't spend your time on it.
8–10	Try it if it fits easily into your family's and preschooler's schedules.
11–13	Try to work it into your schedules.
14–16	Give it priority over other choices.

You'll want to keep in mind a few considerations that are particularly relevant to a preschooler's schedule:

- Although your child may express an opinion as to whether he would like to sign up for a certain class, discovering what sorts of things really hold your preschooler's interest is largely a matter of trial and error.

- All preschool activities require adult time, too. First, there is the time to get your child ready for the activity. Then there is the time to transport her there and back. In addition, many programs require a parent to stay in the room.

- Some classes are designed for parents to actively participate along with their children. If you think you or your child would like for the two of you to spend a little more time together, then one of these classes may be the answer.

- On the other hand, if you feel you could use a little more time in your day without your preschooler at your side, then you may want to steer toward an activity or two that let you go accomplish something else—or just sit quietly and read—while your child expends some energy.

Try to remember that no matter how appealing an activity sounds, if it doesn't fit smoothly into your family's schedule, then it's not the right choice. On the other hand, if the family's schedule doesn't allow time for the preschoolers to have activities of their own, then the schedule needs some adjustment. Allocating time to benefit all family members is always somewhat of a balancing act.

tip Because the average preschooler requires a minimum of 11 hours of sleep a day, whereas the average adult needs only 8 hours, parents should have at least 3 hours a day to spend at home preschooler-free.

To do list

☐ Use the guidelines in Table 8.2 to adjust your preschooler's activities to create a balanced schedule

Striking the Right Balance

Striking the right balance for your family means making sure that the needs and interests of everyone are taken into account and accommodated on an evenhanded basis. In one sense, that's what this whole book is about: organizing the family's schedule so that it works for everyone. Striking the right balance for your preschoolers means making sure that they are not just relegated to tagging along with the rest of the family.

But we don't mean that you have to cram every free moment with a structured preschool activity. For a young person, everything in the world is a new experience. Every task, no matter how repetitious to an adult, is a learning opportunity to a four year old. So, although preschoolers don't always need a structured activity, they do always need time to process what they've experienced throughout the day. In part, this is why young children need more sleep than adults. Some quiet time during the day also helps their learning.

HELP OR HINDRANCE

How many times have you, or another parent or older sibling you know, said something like, "She helped me bake the cookies, and it took me three times longer than if I'd done it by myself"?

A simple adjustment to this way of thinking will help you feel as though your schedule is much more on track. Let's say baking the cookies by yourself would normally take you 30 minutes, but with your child's "help," it takes you an hour and a half. And let's say that you would like to spend an hour of "quality" time with your child every day, but you find that making the time is difficult. Now, instead of saying that baking the cookies took you an hour and a half, why not think of this situation as having spent an hour and a half of quality time with your child and having managed to get freshly baked cookies as a bonus. You've exceeded your goal of time with your child and still managed to bake the cookies!

So, next time you're ready to tell your young child you can play with him after you've dusted the house, remember that preschoolers love to emulate and help you, and then hand him a feather duster. Why is it that he sees vacuuming the carpet, scrubbing the sink, and doing the laundry as fun, and you don't?

After you take into account the amount of time a preschooler needs for sleeping (11–13 hours), eating, and personal care, you'll see that her day can fill up pretty quickly. How you need to structure her time at home will depend on whether she is at home all day, or in preschool, or in preschool and day care, for part of the day. Table 8.2 illustrates how a preschooler's time might be allocated. You should take a close look at your preschooler's schedule to make sure that her use of time is properly distributed.

Table 8.2   A Preschooler's Day

Activity and Target Time	Place	Schedule A (Hours)	Schedule B (Hours)	Schedule C (Hours)
Sleep Target = 11	Home	11.00	11.00	11.00
Personal care Target = 1	Home	1.00	1.00	1.00

Table 8.2 Continued

Activity and Target Time	Place	Schedule A (Hours)	Schedule B (Hours)	Schedule C (Hours)
Eating Target = 2	Home	2.00	1.75	1.50
	Preschool		0.25	0.25
	Day care			0.25
Enrichment activities Target = 2	Home	2.00		
	Preschool		2.00	2.00
	Day care			0.50
Quiet time or nap time Target = 2	Home	2.00	1.75	1.25
	Preschool		0.25	0.25
	Day care			0.50
Structured time Target = 2	Home	2.00	1.00	
	Preschool		1.00	1.00
	Day care			1.50
Self-directed time Target = 2	Home	2.00	1.50	0.50
	Preschool		0.50	0.50
	Day care			1.00
Flexible time Target = 2	Home	2.00	2.00	0.75
	Day care			0.25
Total		**24.00**	**24.00**	**24.00**

Schedule A: Home all day

Schedule B: 4 hours of preschool a day

Schedule C: 4 hours of preschool + 4 hours of day care a day

To do list

- ☐ Select chores for your preschooler that match her abilities
- ☐ Set up a preschool planner

Involving Your Preschooler in the Family Schedule

For your family's schedule to run smoothly, all family members must do their part. Preschoolers want to emulate the older members of the family, which gives you the perfect opportunity to get them involved without any hassle. All you have to do is remember to keep their involvement fun.

Selecting Appropriate Tasks

For you to be successful both in terms of getting cooperation from your child and in terms of getting something accomplished, you'll want to select tasks for your child that match his abilities. Children of preschool age generally have reached a stage in their development at which they have fairly coordinated large motor skills as well as the reasoning ability to do tasks that require matching objects or counting small quantities. They also enjoy most things that involve water. With these characteristics in mind, you can put together a short list of chores for each of your preschoolers. If you need some help getting started, look at the list in Table 8.3. About 15 minutes of chores a day is a good target amount to use as a starting point.

Table 8.3   Age-Appropriate Chores for Your Preschooler

On his own:	With some help:
Pick up toys.	Bathe.
Set the dinner table.	Brush teeth.
Wash the bathroom sink.	Get dressed.
Fold towels.	Match socks.
Put away the clean cutlery from the dishwasher.	Feed the pet.
Put dirty clothes in the hamper.	
Water the plants.	

Things You'll Need

❏ A timer

For a hard-copy preschool planner:

❏ 3- by 5-inch index cards in assorted colors

❏ Stickers, stamps, or pictures illustrating your preschooler's chores and activities

❏ Colored pens, pencils, or markers

❏ A large magnetic surface

❏ Several small magnets

❏ A container for the cards

For a computer-based preschool planner:

❏ A desktop computer with a mouse

❏ Clip art illustrating your preschooler's chores and activities

❏ Drawing software

Giving Your Preschooler a Personalized Planner

Just because your preschooler can't read or tell time doesn't mean he's too young to begin using scheduling tools. Even though he can't look at the clock and tell you if five minutes have gone by, if you set a timer for five minutes, he'll know if he finished the task before the buzzer went off. You may find that he can get the job done in an amazingly short amount of time just to make sure he beats the clock. You can play a game in which you reduce the amount of time you give him each time he does the task until he reaches his most efficient performance. (You may even be inspired to try this technique with your own chores!) Or you can set up a race between you and your child to see which one of you can finish your chores faster.

If you want a system that requires less participation on your part, start by considering that children learn to identify objects and colors before they learn to read. With that thought in mind, set up a system as follows:

1. Select different colored cards to indicate the time period of the day a chore is to be done. For example, blue cards could be used for tasks your child is to complete right after breakfast, and red cards could be used for tasks to be completed while the older children clean the kitchen after dinner. As you can see, one of the keys is to tie the time frame to events that the young child will recognize rather than to a clock.

2. Add stickers or stamps, or draw pictures representing your preschooler's chores to create a card for each task. Be sure to use a card of the color that represents the time frame when you want the task completed.

3. Include cards for activities in which the child participates as well. For example, use a card showing swimming if your child attends swimming lessons or a card showing groceries if your child goes with you to the grocery store.

4. At the beginning of each day, place the cards for that day in a specified place or attach them with magnets to the refrigerator.

5. As your child completes each chore, he should move the card to a storage box. (If you're using a literature sorter as suggested in Chapter 2, "Setting Up Your Planner," you can designate one of the slots for the completed cards.)

note The I Did My Chores! system, shown in Figure 8.1, is designed for children ages 4 through 12. Suggested retail: $19.95. Website: www.ididitproductions.com

Product Note

If your family is using a card system like the one described in Chapter 4, "Dealing with the Necessities of Life," then this setup will parallel the family's system.

FIGURE 8.1

The I Did My Chores! system holds pictures of chores on hooks representing the time of the day that the child is to complete the chores. As she completes each chore, the child removes the card from the hook and places it in the "I Did It!" box.

If your preschooler likes to work with your computer—and more and more young children are computer-savvy these days—you may want to create a special electronic chore chart for her. The principles of using graphics rather than words and of making the chart interactive remain the same:

1. Find clip art to represent the various tasks.

2. Arrange it on a page in a way that indicates when each chore should be done.

3. Set up a simple system for your child to use to indicate that the task has been completed, such as

   • Dragging the image to another area on the page.

   • Deleting the image (make sure you maintain a master copy of the document for reuse).

   • Marking the graphic with another graphic that indicates completion.

Depending on your own level of computer literacy and the amount of time you have, you can decide how creative you want to be in designing the system.

By providing your preschoolers with simple planning tools that work for them, you'll be encouraging them to take an active interest in your family's schedule as well as providing them with a solid foundation on which to build more sophisticated time management skills as they mature.

Chapter Summary

In this chapter, you learned how to tailor the basic techniques for selecting planned activities to the needs of your preschooler, in the context of the overall family schedule. Then you learned how to help your preschooler begin to manage his own time by providing him with a basic, beginning planner that uses the skills he's already developed.

Before leaving this chapter, use the following checklist to make sure you haven't missed a critical step in organizing your family's schedule.

- ❏ Select the structured activities in which your preschooler will participate.

- ❏ Make sure that your preschooler's nonstructured activities complement his structured activities so that he has a balanced schedule that allows for maximum personal development.

- ❏ Double-check that your preschooler's activities don't dominate the family's schedule and that the family's schedule doesn't eclipse the preschooler.

- ❏ Assign age-appropriate chores to your preschooler. (Remember that he'll see them as fun unless you teach him otherwise.)

- ❏ Select a picture-based planner for your preschooler and teach him how to use it.

Preschoolers learn and grow quickly. In the next chapter, we'll look at how you'll need to adjust your family's schedule when you have school-age children.

Planning Around the School's Schedule

"Mom, my science project is due tomorrow, and I need a tri-fold poster board for my display." "Dad, the teacher says I don't have my medical records in the school office so I can't go on the field trip." "I'm starving; I couldn't eat lunch today because the fish sticks in the school cafeteria tasted like cat food!" If you think for a moment that your child's life at school doesn't affect your family's schedule at home, then you're wrong.

And, of course, the key to keeping the school's agenda from causing stress in your home is to plan ahead so you're not caught off guard. You'll want to begin your planning as soon as you can—well in advance of the start of the school year—to prevent as much last-minute scrambling around as possible. In this chapter, you'll learn how to coordinate the school's schedule with your family's schedule and how to help your children learn to manage their own schedules.

Things You'll Need

- ☐ Your children's school calendars
- ☐ Class schedules sent home by your children's teachers
- ☐ Your family's planner

To do list

- ❑ Schedule students' medical appointments well in advance, preferably during the summer
- ❑ Reschedule music lessons and other activities around the school day
- ❑ Request school calendars for future school years

Incorporating School Activities into Your Family's Schedule

Once children enter school, their time no longer belongs to them and their family alone. Just as jobs place restrictions on adults' lives, schools place restrictions on students' lives, and all of those restrictions impact the way the family can schedule its time.

Adjusting the Family's Schedule

When a child is ready to start school, we tend to put all of the focus on how this new phase will impact the child's life. But the first changes you'll really begin to notice probably are the ones that affect everyone. Many families with only preschool children choose to vacation in the autumn months when the weather is cooler, the attractions are less crowded, and the hotel rates are lower. Except for the weather, those advantages exist, in large part, because families with school-age children can't travel then. After any of your children are in school, your family will be unable to vacation then as well. Likewise, a midwinter break to a warm, sunny destination for people living in areas where the winters are very cold or to snowy mountains for families who like to ski may have become a welcome routine. Once the children are in school, you'll be confined to one of the couple of weeks of winter when almost everyone else is trying to get away, too. You can avoid any bad feelings that come with these realizations by taking a super vacation during the summer and booking any winter travels well in advance—after checking the school's winter and spring vacation schedules.

> **tip** Most school districts set their calendars three years in advance. Even if they haven't been published yet, you can find out when the school's vacation breaks have been scheduled by calling the school district's central administration office.

SCHOOL LUNCHES

Even something as simple as eating lunch takes on a whole series of scheduling issues when school enters the picture. The first question to answer is this: Will the student purchase lunch at school or bring a lunch from home?

You and your student should take into account several considerations when answering this question:

* Does going through the cafeteria line at school leave your child with enough time to eat at a reasonable pace? Some cafeteria lines are so long that some students aren't able to sit down with their lunches until five minutes before they need to get back to class.

* Does your student like any of the food available for purchase at school? If not, then packing a lunch every day will be your best option.

* Does your student like some of the food available at school, but not all of it? If so, then you'll want to review the published lunch menu to determine what days your child will buy her lunch and what days she'll carry it. You'll need to factor these choices into your grocery list for each week.

* Does your student like almost all of the food available at school? If so, then you and your student may decide that purchasing a lunch at school—and coordinating the school lunch menu with your family's dinner menu—is the easier solution.

After the decision has been made to pack lunches—and the grocery shopping list and schedule have been adjusted to make sure you have the right foods (and paper and plastic products) available—you still need to decide

* Who will make the lunches? Will one person make the lunches for everyone? Will the same person make all of the lunches every day, or will the job rotate? Will each person make his own lunch?

* When will the lunches be made? Making them in the evening has the advantage of avoiding the morning rush, but it has the disadvantage of making the lunches a little less fresh-tasting come noontime the next day.

* Will the lunches be packed in disposable paper bags or reusable insulated bags? The insulated bags will keep the food better, especially if the lunch contains highly perishable items or needs to be stored in a hot locker, but the student will have to take responsibility for bringing the bag home every afternoon.

With all of these factors surrounding just the scheduling of lunch, is it any wonder that coordinating your family's schedule with the school's schedule requires serious concentration?

You'll find you also have to start scheduling other more routine activities around the school day as well. If you want to avoid having to make your child miss school for doctor and dentist appointments, you'll have to book them much further in advance to get time slots during the more scarce after-school hours. And, even if you're willing to let your child miss school, you'll find it's difficult to

tip   To make the transition to the school schedule easier, change your family's sleeping and eating patterns to match the school-year schedule a week or two before the start of the school year.

make sure that you don't schedule the appointment during an important test, assembly, or field trip.

One way to avoid this type of scheduling nightmare altogether is to plan to make all annual appointments during summer vacation. Early summer appointments are probably easier to get than late summer appointments; plus, they have the added bonus of being taken care of earlier rather than later. Make a note in your planner to book these appointments in January or February to ensure that you can get the dates and times that won't conflict with your other summer activities (camp, swimming lessons, vacation, and so on).

caution   Before rescheduling all of your child's current activities around the school day, don't forget to take time to evaluate whether he should be continuing with all of them on top of his school responsibilities. See Chapter 6, "Participating in Enrichment Activities," for more information on periodically reevaluating scheduled lessons, sports, and other such activities.

While you're at it, you'll want to reschedule private music lessons and other such activities well in advance of the start of school. After-school and weekend spots fill fast, so there's no question that the organized family is the one that will get the most desirable time slots.

To do list

- ❑ Fill out all of the forms the school sends home
- ❑ Schedule back-to-school shopping excursions for clothes and supplies
- ❑ Make arrangements to attend school events
- ❑ Find time to talk about school with your child
- ❑ Set aside time for doing homework

Adding in the School's Schedule

After you've rearranged your family's schedule around the standard school day, you still need to add into your schedule a wide variety of items that are tied directly to attending school:

- Meeting the school's administrative requirements. You'll need to begin this task before the school year by making sure that you've filled out all of the necessary registration forms and provided the school with documentation of your student's immunizations (getting the immunizations first, if necessary) and proof of residency. Then, at the beginning of the school year, set aside enough time to fill out emergency notification forms, student directory forms, teacher questionnaires, and any other paperwork that gets sent home. Finally, set up an ongoing system with time allotted to fill out permission slips and other requests that come home throughout the school year. Designating a place for your students to put forms when they come home from school, coupled with places where you'll put completed forms for each student, will go a long way to keeping this administrative task running smoothly. An occasional reminder to each student to use the system wouldn't be a bad idea either.

- Making sure your student has the right tools. Back-to-school shopping has become a sort of national tradition. Whether your child wears a uniform pre-scribed by the school or a personally selected wardrobe, schedule the time for clothes shopping into your family's planner as soon as you've established your summer schedule enough to know when you'll have a block of time available. Many teachers now send home school supply requirements—or put them on file at local stores—sometime over the summer. As soon as you receive the list—or sooner, if you know when teachers at your school send them out—block out time for this shopping in your family's planner, too. Also, block out time in the evening of the first or second day of school to make another trip to the supply store; no matter how well-equipped your student is on the first day of school, something always needs to be exchanged or added!

- Attending school events. Study the school calendar carefully to see when must-attend events will take place for both parent and student. Look for things such as parent open house, assemblies, awards programs, concerts, plays, other productions, field trips, and parent-teacher conferences. If you're not sure what an event is, don't hesitate to call the school office and ask. If there's an event that you should attend as a parent, make sure you get it into your planner and make the necessary arrangements to take off from work or get a babysitter for younger children. Never assume that your child won't get an award or participate in a project; keep your schedule as flexible as possible around any possible event. Also, if your child is in elementary school, you might want to find out early on if the school offers opportunities for you to volunteer in the classroom, and plan ahead if you're interested. The more years your children are in school, the easier it will become for you to review the school calendar and know what dates and times to enter into your planner.

- Talking about school. Your child needs an adult to talk with about school situations—both the good and the bad. Make sure your schedule and your student's schedule have room in them for these conversations. This time may be as simple to find as talking with your student when you pick her up at school to take her to a music lesson, or you may find that you need to do a little more planning.

- Setting aside time for homework. The amount of time the student needs to set aside for homework will depend on how much the teacher is assigning (which may depend on the student's grade level) and how long the individual student takes to do it. The family can help by scheduling homework time into the family's planner. You can't realistically expect a student—especially a young student—to concentrate on a homework assignment if the rest of the family is doing something that he finds more alluring, such as having a water fight in the backyard or eating fresh-baked cookies.

> **tip** If you live in an area that has year-round school, then slot the school's annual administrative requirements and your family's "back-to-school" shopping into the breaks between terms that are most appropriate to your school's calendar.

To do list

- ☐ Create a visual representation of time for your young student
- ☐ Show your student how to break down long-term projects into reasonably sized steps
- ☐ Choose planning tools with your student to keep track of chores and school work

Helping Your Children Learn to Manage Their Own Schedules

As your children move from kindergarten through the middle school grades, they'll learn many things about many subjects. One important life skill—which is sometimes overlooked in school and sometimes covered quite well—is learning how to manage one's time. As with all subjects, time management is easy for some people and not so easy for others. You can help your student learn to manage her own schedule by giving her the basic understanding and tools she needs to succeed.

Things You'll Need

- ☐ Paper
- ☐ Pen/pencil
- ☐ Scissors
- ☐ Ruler
- ☐ A large sheet of paper or tag board (at least 8 by 15 inches)
- ☐ Your to do lists that you created in Chapter 4

Teaching Scheduling Skills

Early in your child's school years, he will learn to read a calendar and tell time. Probably right about that time, too, he'll start to get homework assignments on a regular basis. No doubt, he'll also be continuing with some enrichment activities outside of school. Plus, he'll probably be picking up a few more chores around the house. This would be an ideal time for you to teach your child some scheduling basics.

Seeing Where the Time Goes

Even though your child can tell time and has a sense of how long minutes and hours are, she may not have a good sense about how much activity will fit into a day. So, she'll think she can play video games until dinner and still have time to practice piano, do her homework, and bake cookies with you—and still get to bed on time. Then when she runs out of time, tempers—yours and hers—flare.

You can help your child understand what went wrong—and how to prevent such situations in the future—by showing her how to construct a *manipulative*—a physical representation of time with interchangeable, movable pieces that represent specific activities and the blocks of time they occupy. Using the manipulative will help your child learn where her time goes. The example in Figure 9.1 shows how the finished pieces will look.

FIGURE 9.1

Representing time tangibly will help your child spot scheduling dilemmas.

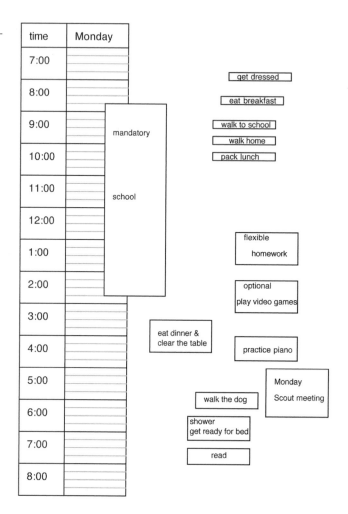

To create this sort of manipulative, follow these steps:

1. Start by helping your child make a list of everything she needs to do. This list will be similar in nature to the to do lists you learned to make in Chapter 4, "Dealing with the Necessities of Life." You'll want to make this list more expansive, though, including everything your child needs to do, including traveling to and from school and all of her activities.

2. Also have your child include on the list everything she'd like to do—activities such as watching TV, playing video games, and playing with her friends.

3. Indicate on the list which days of the week each item needs (or is wanted) to be done.

4. Mark down how long each item takes if it's something your child needs to do or how much time your child would like to spend doing it if it's something she wants to do. Round each time to the nearest 15 minutes (quarter hour).

5. Mark each item as Mandatory (such as going to school), Flexible (such as completing homework), or Optional (such as playing video games).

6. Decide how many hours of sleep your child should get each night, so you can figure out how many hours a day you want her to count on being awake to do things. You shouldn't let anyone in the family schedule so much that getting it done will cut into their sleep.

> **note** When helping your child list how long she will participate in activities to be included on the manipulative schedule, you should consider negotiating some minimums and maximums. For example, you may feel that she should spend a minimum of two hours a week socializing with her friends and a maximum of five hours a week playing video games.

7. For each day, make a strip of paper at least an inch wide and long enough to have an inch of length for every waking hour. In other words, if your child should get 10 hours of sleep a night, then each day's strip would be 14 inches long. (See Figure 9.1 for an illustration.) You can lay out the entire week on one large sheet of paper with seven columns.

8. Write the hours of the day at one-inch intervals down the side of the page.

9. Represent each to do item on a rectangle of paper that's as wide as the columns and a quarter inch long for each 15 minutes of time it will take. If your child needs to do something five days a week, make five separate pieces for that item.

10. Have your child place the pieces into the columns at the times they need to be done.

If the pieces take up more space than the column, then there isn't enough time in the day for everything she wants to do. If this is the case, take a close look at your child's schedule with her. If she's truly overworked, you may want to consider taking away some of her chore duties. If she's not making good choices about how to spend her time, you can help her realize that she'll have to cut out some of her leisure selections. Together, the two of you can also evaluate her extracurricular activities to determine whether any of them should be left off the schedule for now.

> **tip** Even some adults are kinesthetic learners—they learn through touching and moving—and this technique can help them understand their scheduling dilemmas better, too.

If the pieces easily fit within each day, but your child is still having trouble getting everything done, then you'll need to look at motivators to keep her from wasting time. Whatever the case may be, literally seeing how activities fill up time will help your child master the basics of scheduling.

Tackling Long-Term Projects

Another area where you can help your school-age child develop good time management is with long-term projects. Even if you are yourself a procrastinator, you'll know in your head that if you can help your student learn to complete these assignments in reasonably sized increments over time, then you'll all be better off than if he waits and has to race to cram them into the last hours before they're due. Show him how to break down the project into manageable steps:

1. Divide the project into logical parts that can each be completed in about a week and set weekly due dates for each part. (Example: Week 1—pick a topic; week 2—make an outline; week 3—do research; week 4—write a rough draft; week 5—write the final draft; week 6—make the report cover.) Some teachers break down the project for their students and require them to turn in each step for credit. If your student's teacher has done this, then all you need to do is make sure that you help your student keep track of the due dates.

2. Set a plan for each part and enter the required tasks into your planner. (Example: Make sure in week 3 that you schedule a trip to the library to get research materials.) As an aid to your planning, keep asking your student "What else do you need to complete this task?" until the answer is "Nothing."

3. Help your student to stay on schedule by monitoring his progress every day.

Things You'll Need

- ☐ A chore chart your student likes to use
- ☐ A user-friendly individual planner for your student
- ☐ A portable organizer for school papers

Choosing an Age-Appropriate Planner

Although you can jump in at any time to help your children organize their schedules, ideally you'll be building their school-age skills on top of the ones you taught them in their preschool years. To begin, this will mean adding some additional chores that they're now capable of handling (see Table 9.1) and making sure that the method they have for keeping track of their chores is still appealing to them.

Table 9.1   Additional Chores for School-Age Children

Empty the wastebaskets.	Walk the dog.
Clear the dinner table.	Dust the furniture.
Sort the laundry.	Vacuum the carpeting.

If you have a child just entering kindergarten, she'll probably still like the type of chore system we discussed for preschoolers in Chapter 8, "Managing the Preschool Years." In fact, the continuity of a familiar system will probably be very attractive to her. But as children grow and progress through the middle school years, they like to transition to more sophisticated systems. You can help keep chores from getting ignored by looking for the right time to switch your child from a graphic-based system to a word-based chore chart. If your family is using a computer-based family planner, then it's likely that your child will prefer a computer-based chore chart. And, as your child becomes more and more independent, you may find her wanting to take full responsibility for her tasks by keeping track of them in a personal electronic planner.

note Trend Enterprises, Inc., carries a large line of chore charts in a variety of colors and themes for ages five and up. Each set comes with a pad of 25 weekly charts (plus 100 stickers to get you started). Suggested retail: $5.99. Website: www.trendenterprises.com

Of course, by the time your child is in second or third grade, you'll want him to be able to keep track of his school assignments and extracurricular activities in addition to his household chores. Student planners have come a long way since the days of the 3- by 5-inch spiral notebook. Now they come in all shapes and sizes, and with a wide variety of page layouts. You'll want to make sure that you select one that's very user friendly.

note Dr. State's Computer Parent Family Software includes a computerized chore planning and tracking system. Windows-based computer users can download a free 15-day trial. Suggested retail: $19.95. Website: www.computerparent.com

Most of the features that you'll want the planner to have are exemplified in the format illustrated in Figure 9.2. Such planners offer the following benefits:

- Entering information is easy. The student can enter an assignment that will cover a span of days by writing it in once and drawing an arrow or by writing it in across the entire time span. (Some other formats would require that the assignment be rewritten in a separate space for each day.)

- It allows for customization. Although the standard subjects are preprinted, blanks are provided for the student to write in other subjects specific to his course of study.

caution *Brain Wave*

Some schools provide planners for all of their students based on a general recommendation from the company that sells them. Take some time to analyze any planner issued by your student's school, and, if it doesn't work well with your student's planning style, make the effort to find a planner that does.

- A lot of information can be assimilated very quickly. By looking down a column, the student can see everything that is due on a given day. By looking across a row, the student can see all assignments for a certain subject for the entire week.

- There is a "hook." A section on each page containing fun facts or a cartoon gives the student an enjoyable reason for opening the planner.

note *Product Note* The Franklin Covey Middle School Planner (product #25484) uses a layout similar to the one in Figure 9.2. Suggested retail: $8.95. Website: www.franklincovey.com

Although planners with this format are frequently sold as "middle school" planners, there is no reason that they won't work for elementary school children, and savvy high schoolers have been known to seek them out rather than deal with "high school" planners that have a more linear layout.

Children these days get comfortable using electronic equipment—computers, cell phones, and so on—at a very young age. You may find that even your elementary school child wants to use a digital scheduler instead of a paper planner. If he seems able to handle the information without the aid of a more visually based paper planner, then you may want to get him an electronic planner designed specifically for children or possibly even an entry-level adult PDA. Just make sure that he is allowed to enter assignments directly into his digital device while he's at school; otherwise, he's sure to forget some vital information that he needs to enter into his planner.

tip If your child really wants to use an electronic planner but seems to be having trouble keeping track of things, see whether teaching her how to set the alarm function to give her audio reminders will help.

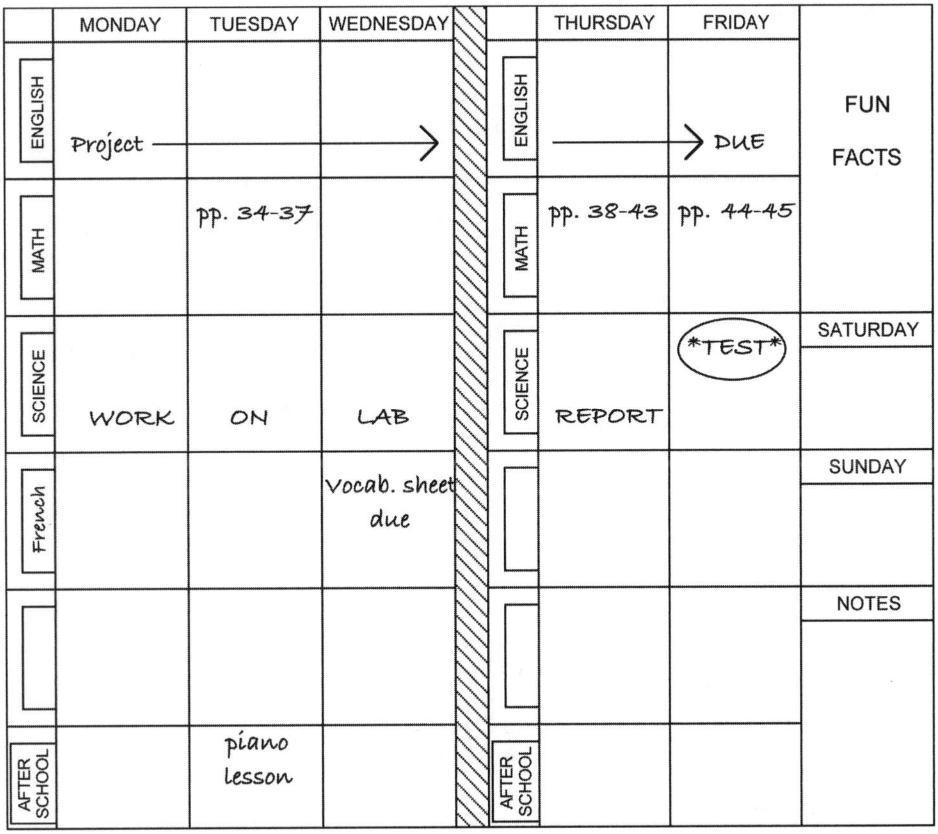

FIGURE 9.2
A planner with subjects down the side and days across the top lets the student enter information with minimum effort and review the day's or week's schedule at a glance.

As a final thought, keep in mind that your child's schedule may look great on paper or an electronic screen, but it will still fall apart if your child has to spend much time looking for misplaced schoolwork. Your student will want a simple system for keeping school papers organized at school, at home, and in between. You'll want to help your student set up a system that keeps work separated by subject and requires a minimal amount of paper shuffling (see Figure 9.3) .

Once your student has an easy way to keep track of both her time and materials, school won't seem like such a burden.

note
The I-Hand SmartCard Message PDA by K-Group Industries is a junior PDA designed for elementary school–aged children. It has a schedule, phone book, alarm clock, calculator, games, and more. Suggested retail: $19.99. Website: www.kgiproducts.com

FIGURE 9.3

This student locker file with removable pockets hangs inside a locker or on a door (left) and folds up into its own self-contained carrying case (right).

note The Pendaflex Student Locker File, shown in Figure 9.3, has five removable pockets to divide school subjects, a clear front pocket, and a built-in hook for hanging on the inside of a locker, on a door, or on a wall. When the product hangs, each pocket cascades down for instant access to student paperwork. The entire file folds into its own compact carrying case. Suggested retail: $19.99. Website: www.esselteamericas.com

Product Note

INCLUDING HOMESCHOOLING IN YOUR SCHEDULE

Homeschooling adds layers of complexity to the family's schedule. But it's really just a matter of making a commitment to the homeschooling lifestyle and then following the same principles of scheduling that we've talked about throughout this book, making sure that you allocate time for preparation, teaching, and following up.

No two homeschooling programs will be exactly alike, but you'll need to incorporate certain steps into your family's planner to keep your schedule running smoothly:

1. Learn your state's laws and regulations regarding homeschooling. Build the time you need to comply with each one into your schedule.

2. Choose one of the four basic styles of homeschooling. The method you select will have a big impact on the activities you need to schedule. Many good books have been written describing these approaches:

   ✳ School at home—This method is highly structured, essentially taking a standard school curriculum and teaching it at home. It seems to work best for people who are highly organized and have children who like structure.

* Unschooling—In this approach, the function of the parent(s) is primarily as a facilitator for learning, letting the subject being explored be determined by the child's current interests.

* Unit studies—This approach takes all (or most) of the standard school subjects and rolls them into a unit centered around one main topic of study.

* Eclectic—This style incorporates elements of each of the other three methods.

3. Develop your curriculum. Your philosophy will determine how prestructured your curriculum will be, and your curriculum largely will determine how you will structure your schooling schedule. Just be sure that you think it through and get it in writing in the family's planner.

4. Determine what evaluation method(s) you'll use:

* Standardized testing—You'll need to arrange for your child to register for the tests and to make sure that they are administered according to the standardized guidelines. Mark the registration deadlines and test dates in your planner.

* Portfolio assessments—You and your student will put together a collection of the student's work to show the student's progress and achievement. Schedule some school time to make the selections at regular intervals.

* Progress reports—You'll write a narrative documenting your student's academic accomplishments and progress. Make sure you have time set aside in your planner to keep this document up-to-date on at least a weekly basis.

* Performance assessments—You and your student will review and assess the student's progress at the culmination of a body of work. Mark down time in the planner at the beginning of a unit to remind you to do this important step at the end of the unit.

5. Complete your record keeping. Even if your state doesn't require records, you'll probably want to document your child's homeschooling for your own information, college applications, and so on. So, don't forget to schedule this important last step in the homeschooling process.

If both parents in your household work, or you have a single-parent household, then homeschooling may require some major rescheduling of your life, including staggering work schedules, self-employment, job sharing, flex time, or telecommuting.

Homeschooling also requires a little more attention to some other aspects of the family's schedule:

* Coordinating socialization opportunities for your children.

* Scheduling time to take care of yourself as an adult, to offset the extra time you'll be spending for and with your children.

* Ensuring that your family schedule clearly distinguishes between school life and home life. Children need to be able to get away from studies. And sometimes they need you to be a parent, not a teacher.

Chapter Summary

In this chapter, you saw that when you have a child in school, you need to adjust the family's schedule so that it blends with the school's schedule. You'll have to reschedule some activities so that they don't conflict with times your child needs to be in school. You'll also want to list all school activities on the family's calendar as soon as possible. School-age children can begin learning time management skills, especially if you take the time to make sure that they have tools that are easy to understand and to use.

Before leaving this chapter, use the following checklist to make sure you haven't missed a critical step in organizing your family's schedule.

- ☐ Adjust the family's schedule to fit around the school's daily schedule and yearly calendar.

- ☐ Enter all relevant dates for school events into your family's planner as soon as possible to avoid schedule conflicts.

- ☐ Help your students understand how much time is needed to do everything that needs to be done.

- ☐ Teach your children how to break down large projects into manageable segments.

- ☐ Together with your children, select planners that they'll find easy and attractive to use.

- ☐ Set up systems for keeping school paperwork neat and organized.

Mastering the school's schedule—both at the family and the individual level—will help your children become more confident and self-sufficient. When they reach the teenage years, they'll be looking for even more independence. In the next chapter, we'll see how you can adapt the family's schedule to accommodate them—and the rest of the family, too.

10

Supporting Your Teenagers

"**W**here are you going?"

"Out."

This classic exchange between parent and teenager sheds a lot of light on the challenges of maintaining a smooth-running family schedule when teenagers are involved. A teenager's desires to be treated as a grown-up and to be independent will cause him to be less than cheerfully cooperative when confronted with a family schedule that is not of his design or choosing. In addition, adolescents begin to feel pressures and add responsibilities from outside the family, and those obligations must be integrated into the teenager's and the family's schedule.

As the teenager matures from child to young adult, his ability to manage his time will become critical to his success and happiness. Your ability to keep him as an active and willing contributor to the family's schedule will be critical to keeping your family's schedule running smoothly.

In this chapter:

* Agreeing where the schedule can bend and where it can't

* Balancing your teenager's freedom with responsibility in the family's schedule

* Developing your teenager's time-management skills

* Finding the right college

Things You'll Need

- ☐ A list of your teenager's chores
- ☐ A list of your teenager's leisure activities
- ☐ Your teenager's work schedule

Agreeing on Schedule Flexibility

Up until the teenage years, children generally are pretty happy if they're told when they have to do things. But with a growing sense of independence, your teenager may quickly decide that such time-dependent scheduling is being "treated like a child." What can you do to alleviate the stress this situation causes without having your family's schedule fall apart? The following sections answer this question and offer information to help you decide when and how to adapt your scheduling to accommodate your family's teenagers.

Reviewing Assigned Chores

You can begin by looking at the chores that you've assigned to your child. Do a lot of them have to be done at specific times? If so, you may want to start to reassign these chores to someone else, especially a younger member of the family. Instead of these chores, delegate tasks to your teenager that require more responsibility. Frequently, these tasks are not as time-dependent. Get buy-in from your adolescent by allowing her to have some input into which family responsibilities she'll take on. Explain that she'll still have to contribute the same amount of effort—or maybe even more—to the family, but that she'll have more autonomy in determining when she'll make the time to do it. Table 10.1 shows you some trades that can be made between time-dependent chores and time-flexible chores.

Table 10.1   Time-Dependent Versus Time-Flexible Chores

Time-Dependent Chore	Time-Flexible Chore
Walking the dog	Washing the dog
Loading the dishwasher after dinner	Chopping vegetables for dinner
Putting out the trash	Mowing the lawn
Picking up siblings after school	Picking up dry cleaning
Placing the family's carryout dinner order	Researching airfares for the family vacation

Of course, sometimes there's just no one else
available to undertake a time-dependent chore.
For example, if you and your teenager are the
only people in your family who are old enough
to take the dog for an afternoon walk, and you
have to be at work at that time of day, then the
chore cannot be reassigned to another family member.

> **tip** A new driver might be willing to take on more chores that involve using the car.

Don't just insist that your teenager conform to a schedule that accommodates this
task. Instead, ask him if he can propose a workable alternative. Perhaps he'd like to
pay the next-door neighbor to walk the dog. Perhaps he'd like to undertake a household project you would have paid someone else to do in exchange for your hiring
someone to walk the dog. Or perhaps he'd like to start a dog-walking service and get
paid to walk other people's dogs along with yours. The solution to which you agree
is not nearly as important as the dialogue that gets you there. When your teenager
has some ownership of the outcome, he'll have a more cooperative attitude about
implementing it.

Unfortunately, sometimes there simply is no alternative to your teenager having to
do a chore at a certain time. You can use these situations as opportunities to reinforce your adolescent's sense of maturity by explaining that having these sorts of
responsibilities is a part of growing up and becoming an adult.

Balancing Leisure Time

Sometimes it seems—at least to the adults—that all teenagers do is sit in front of the
computer, play video games, and watch television. So, naturally, if the family's
schedule is becoming hectic, it's easy to place the blame on these seemingly lazy
members of the family. But don't forget that all family members need leisure time in
their schedules (see Chapter 7, "Planning Other Fun Stuff"). If you think your
teenager is wasting too much time, have an open discussion with her and come to
an agreement about how much time she should be spending in front of a video
monitor. You can set up parameters in a number of ways:

- A single total of time allowed per week or per day for recreational computer,
  video games, and television. For example, 16 hours a week spent among
  these activities in any combination.

- A total time per week for these activities with a daily maximum. For example, 16 hours a week, but no more than 3 hours a day.

- A time limit per week or per day for these activities collectively with specified
  caps on individual activities. For example, 16 hours a week on these activities, with a maximum of 5 hours of TV watching.

- A time limit per week or per day for each of these activities individually. For example, a maximum of 2 hours of recreational computer, 1 hour of video game playing, and 1 hour of television watching per day.
- A trade-off against time spent doing something "more productive." For example, each hour of recreational computer, video games, and television must be balanced against a certain amount of time spent doing homework, studying, and reading.

Whatever the system you work out with your teenager, you can indicate your trust in her ability to manage her life by letting her monitor her own time by filling out a log similar to the one in Table 10.2. If you're using a trade-off system, you'll want to add columns to keep track of homework, studying, reading, and their totals, as well. Getting your teenager accustomed to keeping a log will also promote her understanding of the pace at which time passes.

Table 10.2   Computer—Video—Television Log

Week of _____

	Recreational Computer	Video Games	Television	Total
Sunday				
Monday				
Tuesday				
Wednesday				
Thursday				
Friday				
Saturday				
Total				

To make the use of a log as effortless as possible, try one of the following:

- Compose the master log form on your computer and print out and post a new form each week.
- Compose the master log form on your computer and have your teenager fill out the form on the computer and print—or electronically send—the report for you each week.

- Create the master log on paper, photocopy several weeks' supply, and post a new form each week.

- Create the master log on paper, laminate it, and have your teenager fill it in each week with a dry-erase marker; then you check it and wipe it clean for the start of each week. (Caution: Use this method only if you are confident you'll review and wipe the log clean before the start of each week.)

Acknowledging Your Teenager's Outside Responsibilities

Back in Chapter 4, "Dealing with the Necessities of Life," we saw how one of the first things for which you need to block out time in your family's schedule is the time you must spend earning money at your place of employment. Before long, your teenagers will be seeking employment to earn money, too. They may start with jobs such as babysitting, delivering newspapers, and mowing lawns. Then they'll probably progress to employment with required hours. These jobs are very important to your teen, so you should give them the same sort of precedence as your job in your family's schedule.

To complicate your scheduling endeavors further, teenagers frequently find jobs with early morning, late night, or irregular hours. So, here again, you are presented with the opportunity to collaborate with your teen so that neither you nor he is stuck with an unworkable schedule. Really, the scheduling process is no different from what we've already discussed; it's just that now, in addition to the adults in the family, you have a teenager on your scheduling team.

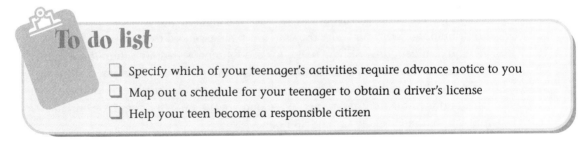

To do list

- ☐ Specify which of your teenager's activities require advance notice to you
- ☐ Map out a schedule for your teenager to obtain a driver's license
- ☐ Help your teen become a responsible citizen

Balancing Freedom with Responsibility

Just because you're willing to make some adjustments to your family's schedule to support your teenager's growing independence doesn't mean that you have to—or should—rearrange your family's schedule to accommodate everything your teenager wants to do. If you've shown respect for your teen's scheduling needs, your teen should show a reciprocal respect for the rest of the family's schedule. You should have an understanding with your teenager that any of his activities which will impact the family's schedule must be communicated and incorporated into your family's planner with as much notice as possible. If a scheduling conflict is apparent, it should be resolved well in advance of the conflicting activities. Because sometimes teenagers don't think broadly enough to realize that their plans affect others, you may want to specify which activities require advance notice. Here are some examples:

- Not eating a meal at home
- Having guests for a meal
- Wanting to use a family car
- Having friends spend the night
- Doing anything that will preclude the teen from completing assigned chores on time
- Needing to use anything that belongs to the family collectively (computer, television, workbench, tools, oven, and the like)

You should decide how much advance notice you need to keep your schedule from being derailed and make sure your teen understands the reasoning behind that requirement.

Learning to Drive

Driving is one of the privileges that accrues in the middle-teen years. It is a major contributor to both your teen's growing independence and responsibility. These days, having a student driver in the house takes a lot more scheduling than it did in the past. In addition to a driver's education course that involves classroom and in-car training with a certified driving instructor, most states also require the student's parents to ride in the front passenger seat alongside the student driver for a specified amount of time, usually around 50 hours.

To see your student successfully through the process to licensed driver without any scheduling crises, you should plan ahead and set aside time in your planner to accomplish each of the following steps:

1. Find out your state's driver's license requirements. This first step is a good task to assign to your teenager. He'll already have some idea from school, and he probably can get any additional information he needs from the Internet. Try to get this information well in advance of the time your teen can actually begin the process so that you can plan ahead.

2. Coordinate your calendar with your teen's if she needs to appear in person to get a temporary permit so you're both available when the registrar is open. Also, double-check that your teenager has all her paperwork in order (birth certificate or whatever else is required) so that you won't have to make a second trip. If your student has to take a written exam before getting her permit, make sure you've planned that time into your schedule.

3. Phone your insurance agent before you allow your teen behind the wheel to make sure your policy covers his driving.

4. Register your student for a driver's education course. Make sure you understand when the class meets and when your student must be available for in-car instruction.

   You can save some time in your own schedule if your student can take driver's education at the school she attends so that you don't have to drive with her to and from class.

5. Create a log to keep track of the hours you spend in the passenger seat while your student drives. Make sure your log is set up to track time spent on highway driving, night driving, parking/maneuverability practice, foul-weather driving, or any other conditions that have specific time requirements.

6. Have your teen coordinate with you and make an appointment for her driving test.

7. Call back your insurance agent after your teen gets his license to double-check that your new driver is covered and to find out whether you can get a reduced rate by submitting proof of driver's education or good grades.

8. Celebrate this milestone with your family! (See Chapter 5, "Celebrating Special Occasions.")

tip   If your teenager has any physical condition that may require special licensing or testing for her to be able to drive, make sure you find out the requirements and schedule the extra steps. Give yourself enough lead time so that your teenager doesn't get left behind by her friends.

WHO HAS THE CAR?

When the number of drivers in your family exceeds the number of motor vehicles in your family, you have the potential for conflicts over the use of the car. If you analyze the situation, though, you'll find that you need only a slight shift in the way you're used to thinking to accommodate the extra driver without a problem.

The excuse that the person who took the car didn't realize someone else needed it will never be valid if you're keeping your family's planner up-to-date. Anyone who's licensed to drive is certainly capable of looking at the family's planner and determining whether another person's activities require a car at any given time. The new driver should be accustomed to figuring out whether someone would be available to drive her to an activity. The same assessment of the family's calendar will reveal whether a car will be free at a certain time.

You also might want to get every driver in the habit of indicating on the family's planner if a particular vehicle will be needed for an activity. For example, if someone has agreed to drive four kids to a soccer game, he should indicate in the planner next to the entry for the soccer game that he'll need the van, not the car.

As with all scheduling conflicts, work out car conflicts well in advance. Walking, biking, carpooling, and public transportation may all prove to be workable solutions.

Accepting the Duties of Citizenship

Your teenagers may think they're adults, but they can usually still use some guidance to assure that they take care of some of their responsibilities that may not be obvious to them. As your teenagers seek employment and reach their late teens, they have several obligations that you may need to remind them to put on their schedules, including

- Registering to vote when they turn 18
- Registering for the draft when they turn 18, if they're boys
- Filing income tax returns when their gross income exceeds the Internal Revenue Service's threshold amount or when they're due an income tax refund

Other activities you may want to help your young adults learn to schedule and implement on their own include banking, investing, securing insurance coverage, and handling medical appointments. Your teenager will quickly develop an appreciation for how complicated adult schedules really are. That realization will help provide her with the motivation to find a good way to keep track of everything.

To do list

- ❑ Review time-management principles with your teenager
- ❑ Reinforce your family's system for avoiding scheduling conflicts
- ❑ Help your teenager select a stylish individual planning tool
- ❑ Show your teenager how to use the features of her planner that most match her preferred and dominant learning modalities
- ❑ Encourage your teenager to switch planning tools if a different planner will work better for him

Building Serious Time-Management Skills

Throughout this book we've focused on the importance of managing your time and your schedule—both for your family and individually. We've shown you ways to teach the basics of time management to your preschoolers and young school-age children. You'll want to impart the same skills at a more sophisticated level to your teenager.

note Some teenagers will have a natural talent for organizing and scheduling and won't need much help. Other teens will need to be guided step-by-step.

Explaining the Basics

You'll probably have more success focusing your teenager's attention on time management if you keep the discussion as short as possible. Concentrate on the basics:

- Outline goals. Explain how knowing what your teenager wants to accomplish—both now (get a B on the history test) and in the longer term (travel to Europe after graduation)—will shape the decisions he makes about how to allocate his time.

- Schedule each step. Explain how to break down each goal into manageable steps that can be scheduled into a planner. Review Chapter 3, "Creating an Activity Schedule," and the section titled "Teaching Scheduling Skills" in Chapter 9, "Planning Around the School's Schedule."

- Increase effectiveness. Explain the benefit of eliminating anything in your teenager's schedule that doesn't serve a purpose.

- Increase efficiency. Explain how to figure out ways to accomplish tasks using less time, money, and energy.

Then make sure your teenager understands that being a responsible member of the family requires her to consider the family's schedule when creating her own. She should compare her schedule to the family's schedule and, if they are compatible, enter her activities into the family's planner. If the comparison reveals that a conflict may occur with other planned family activities, then she must cooperate to resolve the situation before finalizing her plans. It's only fair that other family members extend the same courtesy to the teenager if her plans have been entered into the family's planner first.

Selecting a Planning Tool

As we've said over and over throughout this book, so much of getting and staying organized depends on matching the right tool to the person's organizing style. You can help your teenager select the right individual planning system by having him fill out the various self-assessment questionnaires throughout this book to determine whether he should opt for

note Perhaps the ultimate in cutting-edge PDAs are PDA wristwatches. Their availability is spotty, but searching the Internet for one may be worth the effort if it will motivate your teenager to organize her schedule.

- An electronic or hard-copy planner
- A daily, weekly, or monthly format
- A horizontal or vertical layout
- The use of color

There is still an overriding factor involved in your teenager's selection of a planner that a parent can easily overlook: That's the trend factor. A planner can be the most highly functional system available and perfectly suited to your teenager's way of thinking, but if it doesn't match with the current style, your teenager will never use it. In today's world, being current when it comes to scheduling tools means that the scheduling device has to be on the cutting edge of technology. Even if all indicators point to your student benefiting from a paper planner, your teenager probably will want—almost need—to have a PDA. Along those lines, smartphones—cell phones that also include wireless Internet access and PDA operating systems—are growing in popularity.

 **caution** If other members of your family also have PDAs, make sure that they all run the same operating system so that you can share software and synchronize some of your information. Plenty of smartphones run the Palm or Microsoft Pocket PC operating systems, but the majority of them run the Symbian operating system, which is generally not available for standalone PDAs.

Should you be frustrated if your teenager insists on a digital planner when you believe a paper planner would be a better choice? Not really. Because your teenager likes the tool, he'll spend the extra time needed to make it work for him. In the meantime, he'll be learning the fundamentals of time management that he can use no matter what type of planner he chooses to use in the future.

You can help your young adult get the most out of her digital device by encouraging her to use the features that work best with her learning style. Here are some examples:

- If she's the type of person who remembers things better by writing them down, have her master entering information into her PDA using the graffiti writing tool. (See Figure 10.1.)

FIGURE 10.1

People who remember things better by writing them down will want to make notes using their PDA's graffiti feature.

- If she learns better from illustration rather than the written word, make sure that her PDA contains drawing software. (See Figure 10.2.)

FIGURE 10.2

For some visual learners, drawing software will provide added functionality on a PDA.

- If she forgets to look at her planner for information, teach her how to set the PDA's alarm to remind her to do things.

As a parent, you must accept that if a trendy organizing gadget wasn't a good fit in the beginning, its novelty will wear off and your teenager will need to select a scheduling planner that's a more natural match. Remember that, despite their name, middle school planners are often ideal through all of a student's school years (see

note   PDAsoftnet's
Student Log V 1.0 software for the Palm OS includes a sketch pad for quick drawing along with the ability to sort the student's schedule by subject or day. Both PC and Mac computer users can download a free trial version. Suggested retail: $9.99. Website: www.pdasoftnet.com

Figure 9.2 in Chapter 9). You can continue to support your teenagers in their move toward independence and responsibility by helping them understand that finding the right planner, despite peer and marketing pressures, is a personal choice.

To do list

- ☐ Enter all applicable deadlines into your family's and your student's planners
- ☐ Schedule and plan college campus visits
- ☐ File your income tax returns as early as possible in your highschooler's senior year
- ☐ Use the Internet to locate colleges and scholarship opportunities
- ☐ Block out several days for packing and moving to campus

Finding the Right College

More than four million families in the United States have at least one student enrolled in college. If you have a highschooler who is interested in pursuing higher education, then finding the right college is a major decision that requires a lot of time and is deserving of some special attention when it comes to organizing your family's schedule. If you and your student follow the timeline in Table 10.3, you'll be well on your way to a successful college search and application process. Schedule all of the appropriate items into your family's planner and keep in mind that many of the steps take hours or even days to complete.

Table 10.3   College Search Timeline

Junior Year of High School

October	Take PSAT.
March	Register for April ACT.
	Register for May SAT.
	Review practice ACTs and SATs.
March/April	Get preliminary college ideas with guidance counselor.
	Visit colleges during your high school's spring break.

Table 10.3   Continued

Junior Year of High School

April	Take ACT.
	Plan senior year course selection.
	Register for June SAT or SAT II.
	Review practice SATs or SAT IIs.
May	Register for June ACT, if you didn't take April ACT.
	Take SAT.
June	Take SAT or SAT II.
	Take ACT, if you didn't take April ACT.
July/August	Visit colleges.
	Request college application forms.
	Request financial aid forms.
	Construct a personal and academic résumé.
	Prepare for possible college admission interviews.
	Prepare for college admission essay questions.

Senior Year of High School

September	Check deadlines for ACT and SAT October and November retakes.
	Get college applications you haven't yet received.
	Check Early Decision/Early Action deadlines, if applicable.
	Request personal recommendations from teachers.
	Start to obtain scholarship information and make a note of deadlines.
October	Check application deadlines.
	Complete Early Decision/Early Action application, if applicable.
	Take ACT and SAT, if necessary.
	Follow up with teachers to complete personal recommendations.
	Continue to complete and submit scholarship applications.
December	Turn in applications to your high school office for processing.
	Retake SAT or SAT II, if necessary.
	Get FAFSA and CSS/Profile financial aid forms.
	Continue to complete and submit scholarship applications.
January	Complete and mail FAFSA and CSS/Profile.
	Continue to complete and submit scholarship applications.
February	Continue to complete and submit scholarship applications.
March	Continue to complete and submit scholarship applications.
April	Revisit colleges where you've been accepted, if necessary.
	Select your college and send your deposit.

Here are some pointers to help you integrate this project into your regular schedule:

- Consider that a trip visiting college campuses may have to replace your usual family vacation. If you have younger children in your family, this may be the year to send them off to camp (in the summer) or to visit relatives (during spring break or in the summer) instead of having them tag along. You and your highschooler need to be paying attention while you visit the campuses, and younger children will become bored quickly. The following checklist will help you and your student get the most out of a campus visit:

  - ❑ Call ahead to find out times and starting points of campus tours.
  - ❑ Talk to students; they're a great source of information.
  - ❑ Visit one or more classes.
  - ❑ Meet with a professor, especially if your student has decided on a major.
  - ❑ Visit a dining hall; try out the food and take a look at the students.
  - ❑ Go inside the dormitories.
  - ❑ Ask questions.
  - ❑ Meet with an admissions counselor.
  - ❑ Meet with a financial aid representative.

- You might want to accelerate your usual schedule for filing your family's income tax return because the standard financial aid forms (FAFSA and CSS/Profile) are due in January and you'll need to have your tax returns completed before you can fill them out.

- Your student can use a college locator questionnaire on the Internet, such as the one at www.collegeboard.com, to narrow his search of colleges to ones that have the characteristics he prefers.

- Your student can get a head start on writing her college application essays by downloading the Common Application from the Internet at www.commonapp.org in the summer before her senior year. Just be aware that although the Common Application was designed so that this one form would serve as an application to many colleges and universities, most of the better schools also require students to fill out a supplemental application that usually includes even more essays.

- If you and your student are serious about tapping into independent scholarships to fund his education, your student can fill out a profile on the Internet at www.fastweb.com. Then this service will email him information about scholarships for which he can qualify, along with information about where to download the scholarship application and when it must be submitted.

> **tip** Any time there's a deadline in the application process, enter it in your planner along with a reminder one week in advance of the deadline.

Finally, when it's time for your student actually to head off for his first year on campus, you'll be faced with another scheduling challenge. Make sure you set aside time for both parent and student to go on several significant shopping excursions to procure everything your student will need. Also set aside a day for packing and another day for moving, together with the right amount of travel time.

note "The Ultimate College Checklist" by Diana Zimmerman is part of the "How Am I Supposed to Know That?" booklet series. It contains a thorough checklist to help your student move to college with everything she needs. Suggested retail: $6.00. Website: www.solutions4organizing.com

Chapter Summary

The teen years are a time for the young adults in your family to become more independent and take on more responsibilities. You can maintain a less stressful family schedule if you adjust your teenagers' chores to fit their mindset while, at the same time, reaching an understanding with them that, as members of the family, they have an obligation to support the entire family's schedule, not just their own. You can help them become successful in their independence by teaching them the skills they'll need to develop and maintain their own schedules for the rest of their lives.

Before leaving this chapter, use the following checklist to make sure you haven't missed a critical step in organizing your family's schedule.

- ❏ Reassign chores so your teenagers are given fewer time-dependent tasks.
- ❏ Set up parameters to assure your teenagers make balanced use of leisure time.
- ❏ Adjust the family's schedule to accommodate your young adults' outside obligations.
- ❏ Teach your teenagers how to coordinate individual activities with the family's schedule.
- ❏ Plan time in the family's schedule for your teenagers to learn to drive.
- ❏ Establish procedures to assure that no one in the family is stranded without a car.
- ❏ Remind your teenagers of new responsibilities they must remember to schedule.
- ❏ Explain the basics of time management to your teenagers.
- ❏ Support your teenagers' choices of individual scheduling tools.
- ❏ Invest the time and effort to find the right colleges for your highschoolers who want to pursue higher education.

Although the years sometimes seem to fly by, many years pass from the time you start your family to the time that you no longer have children in the house. During those years, the focus is largely on the children. But the adults in the family are important, too. In the next chapter, we'll focus on organizing the family's schedule so that the adults have time to do more than just take care of everybody else.

Balancing Life for the Adults

Y ou've probably heard the adage "Do as I say, not as I do." This chapter is meant as a reality check to make sure that you haven't been busy organizing everyone else's schedule while somehow keeping yourself outside of the peace you've been creating. Because you're an adult who feels a duty to nurture and provide for your family, it's only natural that you would put yourself last. But, in the end, this approach is counterproductive: You'll ultimately set a poor example; plus, you'll be too cranky and tired to do a very good job of taking care of your family. So, in this chapter, we'll have a little refresher course to help the adults in the family reduce their stress and improve their lives by organizing their own schedules.

Things You'll Need

- [ ] Your family's planner
- [ ] Your personal planner

Leading the Way for the Rest of the Family

You can't realistically expect the planner system you worked so hard to select and set up to work if you're sabotaging its cooperative nature by not using it yourself. How long do you expect your children to check the schedule when they're making plans if you aren't keeping your part of the schedule up-to-date? How long before your older children stop entering their plans into your family's planner if you never bother to check it before making plans that turn out to conflict with the information they've taken the time to post? If the system is going to work, everyone must share in its use with the same level of commitment. As an adult, you are responsible for setting the standard.

It's also your responsibility to establish and implement a vision for your family's collective life. So, while your teenager might set a long-term goal of getting a summer job, you must plan more broadly for major changes such as buying a new car or maybe even a new house. And now that you have your family's day-to-day schedule honed, you should feel confident in your ability to apply the same organizing skills to planning such an event. The techniques we discussed back in Chapter 3, "Creating an Activity Schedule," for creating an activity map, to do list, and timeline

note The Bound to Be Organized Sidetracked Home Executives Planner is a hard-copy planner designed specifically to help someone who's primarily in charge of running a family household to manage the family's schedule and maintain balance. Suggested retail: $99.95. Website: www.shesintouch.com

Product Note

and then scheduling the steps into your family's planner work equally well for large projects as they do for less complicated activities.

Don't forget to select an individual planning tool—hard copy or electronic—that fits your needs and style.

Perhaps you're still conflicted on your choice of a personal organizer because you prefer to take notes with a pad and pen, but you also feel you need to manipulate your information electronically. Even this sort of quandary isn't a valid excuse in today's world! Some currently available products combine input that appeals to a kinesthetic and visual learner with output that has the flexibility of digital technology. For example, you can get a ballpoint pen that writes on specially encoded paper so that when you then place the pen in a dock attached to your computer, it will transfer information exactly as you wrote or drew it. When you select different check boxes on the paper, the information automatically will be entered into your electronic address book, calendar, email, or wherever else is appropriate.

note The Logitech io2 Digital Writing System, shown in Figure 11.1, writes like a regular ballpoint pen on specially formulated paper from Mead, Post-It, and Franklin Covey, and then transfers your writing through a dock to your Windows-based computer. It's compatible with software programs such as Microsoft Outlook and Lotus Notes. Suggested retail: $199.99. Website: www.logitech.com

Product Note

MAKING THE MOST OF THE DAILY COMMUTE

Unless you belong to one of those rare families in which the adults all work from home, at least one person in your family has to deal with the time required to get to and from work every day. In the United States, the average daily round-trip commute takes 52 minutes; that's 4 hours and 20 minutes a week.

If you can somehow make that time do double-duty, the rest of your schedule could be loosened up significantly. The following lists offer some suggestions.

If you drive to work by yourself

* Listen to the news on the radio and forgo watching television news or reading news magazines.

* Listen to music on the radio; music is known to stimulate important brain activity.

* Complete errands that are on your way so that no one has to spend time retracing your route later.

If you carpool to work

* Socialize with your colleagues while you're in the car so you can have a few more minutes of produc-tive work time at the office.

* Listen to the news or music, either with everyone else or using earphones.

If you take public transportation to work

- ❋ Get your exercise by walking to and from the train/bus stop; walking will clear your mind and you won't have to spend time exercising later.
- ❋ Catch a few extra minutes of sleep, if you're still not getting enough at night.
- ❋ Read the newspaper, a book, or a magazine for information or pleasure.
- ❋ Listen to the news or music using earphones.
- ❋ Complete errands that are on your way during the walking portion of your trip.

Making Sure You Don't Get Lost in the Kids

We hope that you took the advice in Chapters 6, "Participating in Enrichment Activities," and 7, "Planning Other Fun Stuff," so that by now the schedules for the adults in your family include

- Enrichment activities—Structured classes or activities on topics of interest
- Hobbies—Enjoyable pursuits in which you get absorbed for hours at a time
- Socializing—Getting together with people outside of your family
- Free time—Moments of peace that spark energy and creativity
- Sleep—Adequate rest so you can function optimally when you're awake

Still, we know that there's a tendency to make these facets of the family's schedule the first to go when time gets tight either because of outside pressures from work or another family member who wants to add an activity. But no one looks out for the well-being of the adults if they don't look out for it themselves.

One way to ensure that you'll take time out from your family duties is for you to volunteer your time doing something you enjoy. By making a commitment to someone outside of your family, you'll create a sense of obligation that will cause you to be more diligent in following through. Whereas dropping an activity you enjoy is easy

tip *Time Optimizer*

Don't wait up! Instead of waiting up and losing sleep to see whether your teenager gets home safely and on time, try this technique:

1. Agree on the time by which your teenager is to be home.
2. Set an alarm clock just outside your bedroom for the agreed curfew time.
3. Instruct your teenager to turn off the alarm setting as soon as he returns home.

If your teen fails to meet his responsibilities, the alarm clock will wake you up, and you can deal with the situation. On the other hand, if your teen gets home on time and disarms the clock, you won't have to interrupt your good night's sleep.

when you're the only one affected, you'll be hesitant to drop the activity when others are depending on you.

Another practice the adults in the family can establish to make sure that all of their time isn't consumed by work and kids is a weekly adults' night out. Make ongoing arrangements for the children on the same night of every week. Preferably, the children will go somewhere away from the home so that even if the parents don't have anyplace in particular to go, they can have the evening free. The key to making an adults' night out work is getting it into your family's planner and not changing it for any other optional event that may come along.

caution After you establish a reputation for being a dependable volunteer, you'll be asked to donate even more time. You must be realistic in how much volunteer time your family's schedule can allow. Practice saying "no"—politely but firmly—so you don't get caught off guard.

FREE BABYSITTING

If you're looking for alternatives to traditional paid babysitters, consider the following suggestions:

* Grandparents—If your children have grandparents in town, chances are both the children and the grandparents would like to be able to spend some time together without you. If the children are young and/or don't need to be at school the next day, perhaps they can spend the night and be picked up the next morning. That way, you can stay out late without having to be concerned about the children's or the grandparents' bedtimes.

* Family and friends—If you have relatives or friends who also have children, you can arrange to have them watch your children one evening in exchange for you watching theirs another one. Again, if the children can spend the night, too, then you can extend your evening out a little later. If all of the children attend the same school(s), you may even be able to continue this arrangement during the school year.

* Community programs—Sometimes finding an alternative to paid babysitters is just a matter of finding an evening program in which your children can participate while the adults do something elsewhere.

Achieving Balance

A family's schedule will stay organized when everyone in the family is committed to it. And that commitment will develop if everyone in the family has a sense that the schedule is fair. This sense of fairness will exist when

- You've assigned everyone in the family an appropriate share of the work.
- You've given everyone's interests an equal amount of attention.
- Your expectations of how much the family will accomplish are not impossible or unreasonable.
- Everyone knows that you've planned the schedule carefully, you update the schedule regularly, and you'll adjust the schedule if there's a good reason to do it.

You therefore should work to balance two different aspects of your family's schedule: the mix of each individual's activities and the distribution of activities among the family's members.

 tip Here are four quick ways to free up time:

- ✳ Stop watching daytime television.
- ✳ Take advantage of free services such as in-store gift wrapping and automatic payroll depositing.
- ✳ Establish a separate email address to use for non-personal contacts.
- ✳ Concentrate on what you're doing instead of talking on your cell phone at the same time.

Chapter Summary

In this chapter, you saw how important it is for the adults in the family to embrace the principles on which an organized family schedule is based. You have to lead by example in setting up the schedule and using the schedule. Most importantly, you need to make sure that your needs as an individual adult are included and valued in the family's plan, not just by the other family members but by yourself as well.

Before leaving this chapter, use the following checklist to make sure you haven't missed a critical step in organizing your family's schedule.

- ☐ Set the standard by using your family's planner.
- ☐ Establish and implement the family's long-term direction.
- ☐ Continue to increase your efficiency.
- ☐ Value adult activities equally with the children's activities.
- ☐ Review your family's schedule to make sure it stays balanced.

Now that you have the family's schedule organized and life running smoothly, what could possibly upset your plans? For millions of families, the sudden need to care for an elderly relative creates new demands on their time. In the next chapter, we'll look at ways to integrate these new responsibilities into your family's schedule without having to redo it entirely.

Dealing with Eldercare

12

More people are living longer lives. This advance has resulted in more people who must care for both their children and their parents—the so-called "sandwich generation." In many ways, caring for an elderly relative is no different than caring for any other family member: It's a simple matter of making sure someone takes care of the elder's needs and wants.

On the other hand, several aspects of eldercare set it apart from child care or personal care:

- A role reversal takes place. Many people—whether the person needing care or the person providing care—find it difficult to accept that an adult who was once self-sufficient and nurtured others now needs help.

- The need may arise suddenly. Unlike the expected arrival of a new baby, you rarely expect the events—or the timing of the events—that result in the need for eldercare.

- The ultimate outcome is not desirable. The need for ongoing care signals that the elder has entered a state of decline that, for the caregiver, can be emotionally draining.

Dealing with the psychological aspects of finding oneself in the role of caregiver is important, but it isn't the focus of this book. What we'll discuss here is how to adjust your family's schedule to handle your new responsibilities. You'll probably find that from a time-management standpoint, eldercare isn't as difficult as you thought it would be. In fact, a recent survey by the American Association of Retired Persons (AARP) concluded that family caregivers as a whole were less stressed, more self-assured, and more at ease in their roles than not.

Things You'll Need

- ❏ Your family's planner
- ❏ Your individual planner
- ❏ Your banking statements and bills
- ❏ Your elder's banking statements and bills

Finding Time to Care for an Aging Relative

How much time you'll need to spend on your caregiving endeavors will depend on several factors including how much help your elder needs, where your elder is living—in his own home, in your home, in a retirement community, or in a senior care facility—and how much of the care you'll provide personally. On average, a caregiver devotes 18 hours a week toward assisting the elder. Our goal here is to show you some practical ways to work this new time commitment into your schedule, as well as some creative ways to handle your added tasks more efficiently.

To do list

- ❏ Assess what help your elder needs
- ❏ Determine tasks and frequencies
- ❏ Schedule the tasks in your planner

Determining Eldercare Needs

The fundamentals of scheduling remain the same in an eldercare situation as they are for any other aspect of your life. You'll want to take some time to assess the extent of the eldercare that's needed and then follow the techniques you've learned throughout this book, creating to do lists, assigning frequencies and time frames to tasks, and then scheduling the items into your family's planner.

- If your situation involves a parent or relative who is still living in her own home, you may find that you have a list for running her household that is almost parallel to the one for your own household.

- If your elder is living in your home, you won't have many additional household tasks at all. You'll want to treat the elder's needs the same way you treat everyone else's in the family. You should schedule time for personal care, enrichment activities, hobbies, socializing, and free time. If the elder can't be left alone in the house, you'll have to make arrangements for the times you'll be away the same as you would for a young child.

- If your elder lives in a retirement community, an assisted-living facility, or a nursing home, you'll want to make your to do list with a clear understanding of what your care responsibilities are.

> **tip** As your elder's sight, hearing, mental acuity, or mobility diminishes, safety becomes an increasing concern. If you're responsible for your elder's living environment, make sure you have replacing smoke and carbon monoxide detector batteries scheduled as a task in your planner every six months. If your elder doesn't have these detectors, make sure you install them right away.

Adjusting Your Family's Schedule to Accommodate Eldercare

Just as any new undertaking—having a baby, starting school, moving to a new home—requires a reevaluation and adjustment in your schedule, so will the addition of eldercare responsibilities. You may find that you need to reallocate the chore load among your family members. If so, look for ways to make the new tasks seem as minimal as you can. For example, you may find that some members of your family would be happy to trade in some household chores in exchange for helping more with the elder's personal care, whereas other family members would rather do the housework. Allocating the tasks according to these natural preferences will keep your family's collective stress lower. You may also find that you need to do some explaining—or negotiation—with your elderly relative. For example, she may have always scrubbed the kitchen on Monday, but if someone in your family has time to do it only on Saturday, then she'll have to cope with the change.

If you're helping your aging relative deal with major life changes such as selling a home and downsizing or moving to a retirement facility,

> **tip** Grandparents love to spend time with their grandchildren, and older people really enjoy music—especially if their hearing is still good. If you have a child who is taking music lessons, you can have him practice with his grandparent as an audience. He'll accomplish three things at once: visiting with his grandparent and practicing his instrument; plus, because he'll be keeping your elder company, you'll be free to do other things during that time.

then you may need to suspend some of your regularly scheduled activities for a while. You may also need to ask your employer to make some workplace accommodations for you, such as changing your work hours or adjusting your workload. If you take the time to create a preliminary schedule of what you need to do for your elder, then you'll have a realistic idea of what adjustments will work.

tip Many businesses—grocery stores, pharmacies, dry cleaners—provide delivery services if you ask. Using services that deliver to your elder's home has the added benefit of having people who check on the well-being of your elder in the normal course of their work.

CONSOLIDATING TASKS YOU HAVE IN COMMON

To be more efficient—which not only will save you time but also reduce your stress—look for ways to consolidate some of the tasks that you need to do for both yourself and your elder. Here are some examples:

* Banking. If you're handling your elder's banking—or even just helping him with it—consider switching his—or your—accounts so they are all at the same bank and you can take care of all of the banking with one trip. You may also want to sign up for online banking if it suits your style and helps your schedule. You'll still want to have both of your accounts at the same bank so you'll have to deal with only one system.

  * Bill paying. Ask companies—credit card, utility, insurance, and so on—to adjust the monthly payment dates on your and your elder's accounts to fit your schedule. Also, consider opting for online or automatic bill-paying options if they'll save you time.

  * Grocery shopping. Shop at the same store as your elder so both of you can do your shopping on the same trip. If you'll need to unload groceries at your elder's house before taking your groceries home, keep an insulated container, such as a cooler, in your car to keep your highly perishable items cold.

  * Personal grooming. Use the same hairdresser or barber as your elder and schedule your appointments at the same time.

  * Preparing meals. When you're cooking for your family, prepare and freeze an extra portion for your elder.

Things You'll Need

- ❏ The names and phone numbers of your elder's doctors
- ❏ A complete list of your elder's medications
- ❏ Your elder's medical insurance information
- ❏ Your elder's local phone book
- ❏ Extra keys to your elder's residence

Managing Medical Situations

Probably one of the most distinct aspects of eldercare is that you'll have to handle an increasing number of health-related situations. These events can be quite stressful, so you'll want to do everything you can to plan your schedule so that they go as smoothly as possible.

To do list

- ❏ Introduce yourself to the staff at your elder's doctors' offices
- ❏ Purchase an accessory that makes it easier for your elder to get in and out of your vehicle, if your elder and you can benefit from such a device
- ❏ Make sure you understand your elder's medications
- ❏ Create a chart of your elder's medication schedule, if he's taking multiple medications
- ❏ Set up a system to remind your elder to take and reorder her medications
- ❏ Write your own step-by-step instructions for filing your elder's medical insurance claims
- ❏ Plan ahead for medical emergencies

Making Doctor Appointments

You can develop a real ally by getting to know the people in your elder's doctors' offices who handle the appointment scheduling. Help them to help you by

- Letting them know that you need to be included in any appointment changes because you're the one who'll be bringing your elder
- Explaining what days and times work with your schedule

- Giving them your phone numbers so they can reach you with a minimum of effort
- Telling them if a particular time of day is more difficult for your elder

MORE PRODUCTIVE DOCTOR VISITS

Take as much relevant information as you can when you go to the doctor:

* Make a list of any problems or concerns your elder is having so that you don't forget to mention them.

* Get a printout from your elder's pharmacist of all of the medications that your elder is taking. You may need to have your elder sign a medical release form before the pharmacist will give you this information. If you can't get your elder to sign the form, ask the pharmacist to fax the information directly to the doctor's office.

* Get your elder's medical records from other doctors whom she's seeing. Again, you'll probably need a signed medical release form, or you'll need to have the information faxed directly to the doctor.

* Have your elder's medical insurance information. Ask your elder if she has an insurance card. If she's not able to supply you with current information, keep a watch on her mail for statements from the insurance company.

If your elder has decreased mobility, transporting him to and from the doctor—and on errands—can require added time, energy, and patience. You can purchase an accessory to make getting into and out of the car easier for both of you. The accessory can be as simple and inexpensive as a seat cushion that swivels or as sophisticated as a factory-installed seat designed for the mobility impaired. With the growing population of senior citizens, new and more innovative products are becoming available all the time.

note *Product Note* The Swivel Car Seat is a covered soft-foam cushion that rotates 360 degrees on a swivel base so that the passenger can get in or out of any car with greater ease. Suggested retail: $24.95. Website: www.aidsforarthritis.com

Tracking Medications

The elder for whom you're the caregiver is likely taking multiple medications. The instructions for taking them may be quite complicated. You'll want to know the answers to all of the following questions:

- How many of the pills should the patient take?
- How often should he take them?
- Must they be taken with food? If so, is the frequency such that your elder will be eating at the right time?
- Must the pills be taken with water, or is another liquid okay?
- What are the likely side effects? Which ones require you to notify the doctor?
- Will there be any adverse reactions with other medications the elder is taking?
- Can the elder drink alcohol while on this medication? (If no, let the doctor know if this restriction will cause a conflict.)
- Should the elder curtail any activities while on the medication, such as driving, being in the sun, or eating certain foods?
- What should the elder do if he misses a dose: skip it or double up?
- Is there an alternative way to take the medicine if the elder has trouble swallowing it?
- Is there anything else the doctor thinks you should know about the medication?

When you understand the intricacies of the medication regimen, you may find it helpful to create a visual schematic of it along the lines of the one illustrated in Table 12.1. For the medication plan in the illustration, we needed a chart two days long to cover all of the combinations because Med C is taken only every other day. Your chart may be even more complex if your elder is taking any medications that alternate between a higher and lower dosage or that cannot be taken in combination with others.

Table 12.1 Sample Medication Schedule

Medication	Med A	Med B	Med C	Med D	Med E
Instructions	With water only	With food	With liquid	2 hours after eating	Before bed
Dosage	Twice a day	Twice a day	Every other day	Once a day	Once a day
Day 1					
Before breakfast			X		
With breakfast		X			
Mid-morning	X			X	
Mid-evening with snack		X			
Bedtime	X				X
Day 2					
With breakfast		X			
Mid-morning	X			X	
Mid-evening with snack		X			
Bedtime	X				X

Next, you'll need to ensure that your elder is taking the medications according to the schedule. If your elder is still living by himself and handling his own medications, you'll want to be confident that he's remembering to take the medications at the right time—and that he's not forgetting when he's already taken the medicine and double-dosing. You can purchase medication reminders and timers for just about every situation from a simple alarm that reminds the patient it's time for medication to a computerized dispenser that releases only the proper pills at the prescribed times. You can even subscribe to services that will phone you automatically if the elder doesn't take the pills out of the dispenser. Figures 12.1, 12.2, and 12.3 show a range of the timers that you can buy.

note *Product Note* The Casio TMR200-2, shown in Figure 12.1, is a combination pillbox/alarm clock with five compartments and up to five alarm settings per day. Suggested retail: $19.99. Website: www.casio.com

note *Product Note* The Beep 'N Tell Medication Reminder pill vial, shown in Figure 12.2, has an alarm clock in the lid that automatically resets for the next dosage when the cap is replaced. The bottom of the vial contains a voice chip for recording personalized instructions about the prescription. Suggested retail: $69.95. Website: www.epill.com

FIGURE 12.1
You can set this pill case (shown here from both the front and back) to ring or vibrate up to five times a day.

FIGURE 12.2
The alarm clock in the top of this bottle reminds the patient when to take the medication; the voice recorder in the bottom can be used for special instructions, such as "take with a full glass of water."

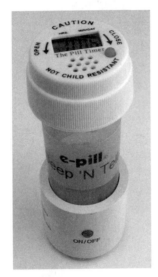

FIGURE 12.3
When it's time to take medication, this device sounds an alarm and rotates into position dispensing the appropriate pills only.

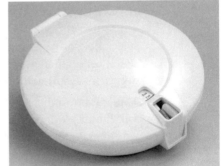

Another scheduling aspect of a prescription medication regimen is making sure that the patient always has a supply of the medications. You can keep track of the refill schedule by making the following entries in your planner as soon as you have the prescription filled for the first time:

note The Med-Time Personal Medication System, shown in Figure 12.3, has 28 compartments and a built-in timer that allows it to dispense pills up to four times a day. Suggested retail: $249.00. Website: www.amacalert.com

- A reminder one week before the medication will run out to order a refill, together with another reminder the day before it will run out

- A reminder two weeks before the last prescribed refill will run out to contact the doctor for a new prescription—and to schedule an appointment if necessary—together with a backup reminder one week before the prescription will expire.

Submitting Insurance Claims

Filing health insurance claims can eat up a lot of your precious time unless you invest the time upfront to create a smooth-flowing tracking system. Your goal here should be to decipher the sys-

caution If you use a mail-order prescription service, you still need to put reminders in your schedule so that you're alerted if the delivery has been delayed or misdirected.

tem once and record step-by-step instructions for yourself so that you won't have to repeat your efforts every time you're faced with a new claim. One way to develop your procedures is to track one claim from start to finish, writing lots of notes to yourself as you go, as follows:

1. Find out what insurance coverage your elder has in place. Chances are, he'll have a primary policy and a secondary policy. Check what the coverages are. If you're having trouble figuring out the coverages, start by asking your elder's doctors' office staff and pharmacist. If you're still not clear, call the insurance carrier. Don't hesitate to call back if you're still confused; maybe you'll get a different representative who will explain the system more clearly. Set aside several hours for this process.

2. Find out how much of the claim process the doctor's office staff or pharmacy will handle. Will they file no claim, only the claim to the primary carrier, or all claims? Make a note about when in the process you'll need to get involved and what the paperwork you'll have at that time will tell you.

3. Get blank copies of all of the claim forms you'll have to file and make several copies of them.

4. As soon as your elder receives a medical service or fills a prescription, enter it, with the date, into a log.

5. Figure out what information goes on what line of the form. Feel free to make yourself notes such as "This figure is found around the middle of the sheet from the doctor's office and is preceded by the letters 'XXYM.'"

6. File the claim and keep track of how long it takes to get a response from the insurance company. When you file subsequent claims, schedule a follow-up reminder in your planner at this interval.

7. If you need to file with subsequent carriers after you receive a response, repeat steps 5 and 6. Save yourself the aggravation of having to decipher the calculations each time by making your own set of instructions with notes such as "Line 8 on the statement from Company A is 80% of the amount allowed, which is shown on Line 3. Enter the amount from Line 8 on Line 12b of the claim form for Company B."

8. If a claim is denied—or comes back for less than the full amount you expected—and you believe the service should be covered, check to make sure that the doctor's office staff coded the service correctly. If they didn't, ask them to recode it and resubmit the claim.

9. After the claim has gone through all of the insurance channels, pay the balance due, if any.

10. Most important is that you create a checklist of the steps you must follow with the insurance coverages your elder has in place and that you keep a log of each claim and where it is in the process.

caution Some older people get nervous about having outstanding medical bills, but it's important that you not pay until you have the absolute bottom-line figure because it's too hard to try to get money back that you've overpaid.

Preparing for Emergencies

When a person's health is in decline, emergency medical situations are inevitable. Emergencies, by definition, require immediate attention and a departure from whatever you had scheduled. You can minimize the disruption to your schedule—and reduce your stress—by preparing as much as you can in advance. You should

- Have emergency phone numbers—doctor, ambulance, hospital, family, neighbor—in your individual planner and with you at all times

- Make sure several people have access to your elder by giving house keys to trusted and caring neighbors

- Keep an up-to-date list of all of your elder's medications with you and posted on your elder's refrigerator so you can tell emergency personnel where to find it

- Have on file with your elder's doctors and hospital whatever legal documents are appropriate to your situation—durable powers of attorney, living wills, and the like

- Know what your options are for home-care providers if they are needed

Take time now to schedule these preparations into your planner and actually make the preparations as soon as you can.

Getting Help with Your Caregiving

Sometimes you may find you don't have the time, skill, or inclination—or you just live too far away—to handle the eldercare by yourself, even with your family's help. You can turn to an array of services for assistance with some or all of your elder's care needs. As a starting point as you try to maintain order in your family's schedule, consider these in-home service options:

- Meals—Your local Meals on Wheels service will deliver hot meals—and sometimes additional cold meals—to your elder. To find the service in your elder's area, enter the ZIP code in the organization's search tool at www.mowaa.org.

- Housekeeping—Hiring housekeeping for your elder is really no different than hiring housekeeping for yourself. In fact, you—and your older relative—may prefer to hire the service for your house and clean your elder's home yourself while you're visiting. If your elder needs help because she's adjusting to newly diminished sight or mobility, you may want to consider having her work with an occupational therapist who can show her how to continue doing many tasks independently.

- Transportation—Many communities as well as private companies provide transportation for senior citizens who are no longer able to drive themselves.

- Personal care and in-home health care—Hospital social workers or the local Area Agency on Aging can advise you of your options for these services. More in-home eldercare services are becoming available all of the time. To find your local Area Agency on Aging, visit the National Association of Area Agencies on Aging website at www.n4a.org.

- Insurance claims—You can hire an independent insurance advocate to handle the insurance claim process for you.

If you need more than the assistance of the preceding in-home services, you might want to consider these alternatives:

- Adult day care—If you need someone to look after your older relative while you're away during the day, you can send him to adult day care. Depending on his needs, you'll choose between a social model day care and a medical model day care.
- Living facilities—As we've mentioned before, senior citizens can move to retirement communities that include independent living, assisted living, and nursing care.
- Care management—If your location, time constraints, or demeanor doesn't allow for you to take on the general responsibilities of eldercare, you can hire a geriatric care manager, a professional who specializes in helping older people and their families with long-term care arrangements. You can find a geriatric care manager in your area through the National Association of Professional Geriatric Care Managers website at www.caremanager.com.

Taking Care of Yourself

If you are the caregiver, probably the last person you think about taking care of is yourself. But you need to take time for yourself. Handling eldercare is not only a lot of work, it's emotionally draining, too. If you let yourself become run down and sick, then you won't be able to take care of the people who need you. Include in your schedule now time to research the respite services for caregivers that are available to you. Then, when you need a break, send your elder on a "vacation" for a week or two—or even just a few days—to one of these facilities. The rejuvenating effect on you will benefit you, your family, and your elder.

Chapter Summary

Whether eldercare continues for a short time or a long time, it almost always ends with a sad event. In this chapter, you learned how to integrate eldercare duties into your regular schedule so that the endeavor doesn't seem like a burden. In the end, the time you spent reworking your schedule in a way that eliminates feelings of resentment by you or your family will serve to have made the time you spent as a caregiver a better experience.

If eldercare is part of your life, then use the following checklist to integrate it into your family's schedule.

❑ Make a list of everything you need to do for your elder.

❑ Assign an estimated time to each task.

❑ Schedule each task into your planner.

❑ Reallocate your family's chores to aid in freeing up time for eldercare.

❑ Find ways to handle your new tasks more efficiently.

❑ Learn the details of your elder's medical care.

❑ Prepare for medical emergencies.

❑ Get outside help if you want or need it.

❑ Take care of yourself, too.

By this point in the book, you should be pleased with the way you've organized your family's schedule. But perhaps one or two things about it don't seem quite as smooth as you would like. In the next chapter, we'll look at how you can make a few additional improvements and how to troubleshoot your system.

Fine-tuning Your Family's Schedule and Planner System

13

In this chapter:

* Adjusting your family's schedule so that it works for everyone
* Troubleshooting your new system

"Mom! It's my turn to use the bathroom, and Jane's still in the shower."

"I hate getting up early to walk the dog. Dick's up anyway; why can't he do it?"

"I just want some time by myself to think!"

We would be closing our eyes to reality if we weren't willing to admit that you may still be able to benefit from some minor adjustments to your family's schedule even if you've followed step-by-step all of the recommendations we've made so far. The reason is that sometimes a schedule that "looks good on paper"—everyone's been given an equal amount of work and a fair allocation of leisure activities—misses some of the nuances that appear as life plays out according to the plan. In this chapter, we'll analyze some of these overlooked details so you'll have an idea of how to eliminate minor rough spots in your family's schedule when they develop. We'll finish up with a look at troubleshooting for those times when your new system seems to have stopped working.

Things You'll Need

- ❏ Paper
- ❏ Pen/pencil

Creating a Schedule Everyone Enjoys

We've spent a fair amount of time considering the different learning styles and preferences of your family members as we've selected a planner and set up your family's schedule. But we haven't looked too closely at personality traits and how they may affect a person's reaction to scheduled activities.

To do list

- ❏ Find out whether you have any "night owls" or "morning larks" in your family
- ❏ Determine whether family members have a preference for indoor or outdoor activities
- ❏ Assess whether family members work better alone or with others
- ❏ Adjust your routines during major short-term projects
- ❏ Revamp your routines after permanent changes in your family's situation

Adjusting for Body Clocks

You're probably familiar with the fact that some people are "night people," whereas others are "morning people." Actually, about 10 percent of the population are morning types, and 20 percent are nighttime types; the other 70 percent don't tend to either extreme. You may already have a good idea of whether you have someone in your family who's a night or morning person, but if you're not sure, you can use the self-assessment questionnaire in Table 13.1 to help you decide. Although a person can adapt somewhat if circumstances require, these tendencies seem to be genetic in nature, which means that, in general, they can't be changed. And, of course, it makes sense that people will feel and function better if they synchronize their required activities to their natural rhythms.

Table 13.1   Self-Assessment Questionnaire: What's Your Best Time of Day?

	Enter the number of your response.
a. What is your favorite meal of the day?	
1. Breakfast	
2. Lunch	
3. Dinner	
b. When do you most often get up in the morning?	
1. Before the alarm clock rings	
2. When the alarm clock rings	
3. After using the alarm clock's snooze feature	
c. When you wake up in the morning, how do you usually feel?	
1. Comfortably warm	
2. Uncomfortably cool	
Total	

If Your Score Is	Then You're Probably
3 or 4	A morning person (lark)
5 or 6	Neither extreme (hummingbird)
7 or 8	A night person (owl)

What might this synchronization mean in terms of your family's schedule? Night owls, who like to stay in bed until the last possible second in the morning, may prefer to take showers in the evening. Because they have a hard time getting energized if they must get up early in the morning, they'll take a lot longer in the morning shower—without even realizing it—and may throw off the entire family's schedule. Particularly if your family has a tight morning schedule, or if everyone showering in succession exhausts your hot water supply, you should consider adjusting your schedule to accommodate anyone's nighttime showering preference.

You may also find using water in the kitchen or elsewhere in the house when someone is showering may throw off the pressure or temperature of the water enough to cause a delay in the bathroom schedule. This detail may seem insignificant, but correcting the disturbance can make your family's mornings much more pleasant. Consider, too, that some people just like to take long showers. What everyone needs to recognize here is that the person does not require more personal care time, but instead he has extended a personal care activity into a leisure activity. The long shower should be shifted to a time in the day when it doesn't disrupt the rest of the family's schedule.

Other activities affected by a person's body clock include exercising and chatting. In general, morning activities go more smoothly for night owls if they follow a routine that entails as much rote behavior as possible. In contrast, morning larks are quick in the morning and can tackle tasks that require alert thinking. You'll want to keep these tendencies in mind when assigning the morning chores.

Considering the Environment

Some people love doing anything outdoors, and other people are more selective about their outdoor activities. The self-assessment questionnaire in Table 13.2 may help you separate these two personalities. By now, it should be obvious to you that if you have an indoor task and an outdoor task that need to be done, and you have one person who likes the outdoors and one person who prefers the indoors, then your schedule will work better if you pair the task with the person who would prefer to do it.

Even if honoring these types of preferences results in a slightly unbalanced allocation of duties, it may be that the perception of imbalance is less than if the duties are mismatched to the personalities. Plus, assigning tasks that are well suited to the person will cut down on procrastination.

Table 13.2   Self-Assessment Questionnaire: Are You an Outdoor or Indoor Person?

	a	b
1. Where would you prefer to eat?		
a. Out-of-doors whenever possible		
b. Indoors if there are bugs outside		
2. Which activity would you prefer?		
a. Sledding		
b. Sipping hot chocolate in front of the fireplace		
3. Where would you rather spend the night?		
a. In a tent		
b. In a hotel room		
Total		

If you answered more *a*'s than *b*'s, you're probably an outdoor type. If you answered more *b*'s than *a*'s, you're probably an indoor type.

Similar factors for you to keep in mind are

- Allergies—Whether indoor or outdoor, no one is in a hurry to do something that will make him sneeze or itch.
- Phobias—People who don't like spiders, heights, or anything else in particular should not be responsible for tasks that involve them. Having these people perform such tasks is neither efficient nor safe.
- Sensitivities—Similar to allergies, some people are sensitive to things such as the sun or certain soaps. If they have to put on sunscreen or protective clothing or gloves to do their work, they'll be less happy about it; plus, completing the tasks will take them longer because of the extra steps.

Working with Other People

Some of your family members may be more people-oriented, either in terms of collaborating with other people or doing things for other people. The self-assessment questionnaire in Table 13.3 will provide you with a quick gauge of this personality trait. People-oriented family members will prefer activities in which other people are working with them or near them. They'll also enjoy doing tasks that they feel help others. Asking them to do things as a favor to you and always saying "thank you" even for tasks they're required to do will keep them in a more cooperative frame of mind.

Table 13.3   Self-Assessment Questionnaire: Are You a People Person?

	a	b
1. Which method of preparing a report do you prefer?		
a. Working with a team to produce a group report		
b. Preparing a research report by yourself		
2. If the compensation were the same, which job would you rather do?		
a. Babysit		
b. Wash windows		
3. If you were attending an out-of-town convention, which accommodations would you prefer?		
a. Sharing a hotel room		
b. Having a private room		
Total		

If you answered more *a*'s than *b*'s, you're probably a more people-oriented person. If you answered more *b*'s than *a*'s, you probably need more time to yourself.

Family members who need more time to themselves will enjoy tasks they can work at by themselves, even if others benefit from the results. You can apply this knowledge to your family's schedule in some creative ways. For example, if you have two children who are both people-oriented, you may find that they'll get their rooms cleaned

note If you took the advice in Chapter 1,"Selecting a Planner," and held off making a final decision and purchasing your planner until you had read through the rest of this book, now is the time to briefly review Chapter 1 and go out and purchase your planner and the supplemental tools to go with it.

with less hassle if you have them work as a team to clean both rooms together. Or they may enjoy cleaning each other's rooms instead of their own. On the other hand, two children who like to work alone may be more motivated by a competition to see who will finish cleaning his own room faster. The point here is that you shouldn't hesitate to tinker with the way you've allocated tasks in your family's schedule until you hit upon the most effective motivators to get things done in the least time with the greatest sense of satisfaction.

Modifying Your Routine

With your newly acquired scheduling skills, you should be able to incorporate most new activities into your schedule without too much trouble. Sometimes, though, new events are of a magnitude that demands a disruption of the normal flow:

- Some of these events are self-contained projects that will require you to suspend your normal routine until they are completed. For example, if your family is buying and moving to a new home, the amount of time you'll need for selling your old house (if you own it); finding, buying, and financing your new house; packing and moving; arranging for changes in utility and mail service; meeting your new neighbors; and so on will probably be enough to keep you from washing the car and attending your book club for a few weeks.

- Other events are life-altering and will require you to revamp your family's schedule. For example, having a baby will add a whole list of new tasks to your daily, weekly, and monthly schedules.

- Still other events are temporary, but yet significant enough to require a retooling of the family's schedule in the short run. These events tend to be unexpected, such as someone in the family breaking a leg or being selected to participate in a four-week foreign exchange program.

Even if you're totally satisfied with your family's current schedule, you must be open to the reality that the schedule is as dynamic as your family and you'll need to modify it regularly.

Troubleshooting Your New System

We hope that you've followed the techniques we've recommended throughout this book and that you now have a planner system and organized family schedule that are working beautifully. But what do you do if the system breaks down? This section provides you with a quick resource to find your problem and the solutions to it.

If the Planner Isn't Working

Problem: The planner doesn't provide enough room for all of the information you need to include.

Solutions:

note The More Time Mom's Family Organizer wall calendar features big squares to write in, along with reminder stickers for important events and a pocket to contain loose paperwork. Suggested retail: $17.75. Website: www.flylady.net

- Consider switching to a planner with a more expanded format. For example, if you're using a monthly planner, perhaps a weekly planner will give you the extra room you need.

- If you're already using a daily planner, you may need to switch to a multi-person daily group appointment book.

- If you really like the format of the planner you're using, you might get a different model that provides more space for each entry.

- If you're using a hard-copy planner, consider whether an electronic one—which will generally have less limited space constraints—may work for your family.

Problem: Your family is forgetting to enter events into the planner.

Solutions:

- Check to see whether the location of the planner is conveniently accessible to everyone and move it if that will help.

- Analyze whether you've selected the right format—hard copy versus electronic—and switch if a change is appropriate.

- Ensure that everyone is using the family's planner as the main repository of scheduling information. Some members may be using individual planners to record events and then forgetting that the information needs to be transferred to the central system. Until everyone gets into the routine of using the central planner, the family's master scheduler should make a point of reminding the other family members; he should have this task scheduled as a recurring item on his own personal schedule.

- If family members aren't keeping track of events at all, make sure that they have individual planning tools that they can carry with them so they can record the information they'll need to transfer to the family's planner.

- If the family's planner is portable, make sure that it doesn't move around so much that people can't locate it when they want to enter information.

Problem: The family's planner keeps getting lost.

Solutions:

- Consider whether you should switch to a wall-mounted planner that can't be carried around.

- Attach a locator device to your planner, similar to the ones found on most cordless phones. Make sure you anchor the base paging unit in a permanent location.

note The KeyRinger remote control locator attaches to any item and responds with a loud tone and a flashing light when the finder button on the paging unit is pressed within 300 feet of the item. Suggested retail: $29.95. Website: www.keyringer.com

Problem: Your family is forgetting to do things that need to be done.

Solutions:

- Double-check whether the item is on the family's schedule. If it's not, then add it.

- Make sure each family member is remembering to check the family's planner and understands which items on the schedule are her responsibility.

- If someone is forgetting to do things while away from home, make sure he has a portable individual planning tool that he keeps updated. If he's forgetting to check the planner, have him set an alarm that will ring to remind him.

- If someone is forgetting to do the parts of a task that are involved in the preparation or wrapping-up phases of an activity, remember that some people see these parts as separate events, so they need to have them scheduled separately.

tip You can schedule some tasks more generally and others more specifically depending on the organizing styles of the people responsible for completing them.

Problem: Some people in your family are forgetting to look at the planner.

Solutions:

- See whether the location of the planner is convenient for them. Remember that the planner should be located where everyone will pass it at least once—and preferably more times—a day. Also, you need to position the planner at a height that makes viewing it easy for everyone.

- Some people need an additional motivator to look at the planner because the thought of facing the day's tasks is not appealing to them. A calendar with a new comic or joke for every day may help. Or you could set up a system of random small prizes or rewards that are given to the first person to find them posted on the planner.

Problem: One person in your family isn't following the system.

Solutions:

- Your planner may not be a good fit for that person's age, learning style, or personality. Instead of trying an alternative to a system that is working for almost everyone, try finding a personal planning tool that will dovetail with the family's system and work for the individual. Consider tools that use more or fewer graphics and colors (for those who are more or less visually oriented), more auditory reminders (for auditory learners), or more interaction from the user (for kinesthetic learners). Consider personal systems that break down tasks into smaller components for those who have trouble focusing on a large project all at once.

- If the person is an age at which she's looking for more independence, try giving her more responsibility or letting her have more input into the overall schedule.

Problem: The planner worked in the beginning, but over time people seem to have lost interest in it.

Solutions:

- The planner may have become so much of a fixture in your house that no one even notices it any more—and, for many people, out of sight is out of mind. Buy a similar planner in a new, vibrant color, or spruce up your old planner with cartoons you change frequently or dollar bills that can be claimed for performing tasks.

- Family dynamics change over time as children grow into young adults. A planner that worked for several years may simply have outlived its usefulness. Assess your family's current situation and select a new planner system that's a good match now.

UNEXPECTED EVENTS AND PLEASANT SURPRISES

No matter how carefully you organize your family's schedule, there's no doubt that occasionally something will happen to upset your plan. It may be an unavoidable happenstance, such as the electrical power to your house being knocked out by a storm or your child waking up with a high fever, that will compel you to alter your schedule. Or it may be a fortuitous event, such as a longtime friend passing through town or your winning tickets to a concert, that will make you want to disregard your schedule.

Surely, it wouldn't be fair if you could deviate from your schedule only when unavoidable problems occur and not when enjoyable opportunities present themselves. As long as your family is accomplishing routine tasks on a regular basis, you'll find that skipping them occasionally won't create much of a break in your day-to-day flow. So, don't let yourself get too upset when circumstances force you to alter your planned activities, and don't force yourself to stick to your plans if something fun unexpectedly pops up. Your schedule is meant to be a tool to help you; you should never feel as though you're a slave to it.

If the Schedule Isn't Running Smoothly

Problem: Your family members are scrambling around at the last minute because they aren't prepared for the next activity.

Solutions:

- Analyze whether your planner has enough space to record all of the preparatory steps. If it doesn't, you may want to get a different planner with more space for details.

- Include reminders of upcoming events on your schedule one week in advance.

Problem: Activities are taking longer than the amount of time you've allotted for them in the schedule.

Solutions:

- Double-check that the time you've allotted is a realistic estimate. To make this determination, focus carefully on the activity and do it as quickly as you can. If you've underestimated how long it should take, then adjust your schedule.

- Determine whether the person responsible for accomplishing the task is succumbing to distractions. People working at the computer can easily get sidetracked for hours surfing the Internet. You can have them set the computer to sound a tone or announce the time at a predetermined interval to remind them to get back on task. Or if you can't take the person away from the Internet, you may find that you need to take the Internet away from the person—and the person could be you! If the computer task doesn't require Internet access, then work on a computer with no Internet connection. If you've chosen to pay your bills online but find yourself getting distracted, then online bill paying may be taking more time instead of saving time; going back to old-fashioned pen and paper may be the more efficient alternative for you.

- If you have children who seem to be taking too long to complete homework assignments, remember that some children study better if it's quiet and others study better if there is music or some other sound in the background. You should make sure that each student's preference is accommodated. Other young students need someone in the room with them to keep them focused; if you have such a student, you might want to try scheduling her homework time in the kitchen while you're preparing dinner or in the living room in the evening while you're reading the newspaper.

- If a family member seems too sluggish to complete a task expeditiously, she may need to get more sleep at night. Or she may need to drink more water; a 2 percent drop in brain hydration can adversely affect her ability to analyze the situation, make decisions, and get the task accomplished.

Problem: There's not enough time in the schedule to have fun.

Solutions:

- Decide what items in the schedule can be eliminated, streamlined, or done by people outside of your family to free up some time.
- Set aside certain blocks of time each week to have fun and don't do anything else during that time. If you start believing that you have less time for "work," then you'll find that you'll get your "work" done in less time.

Problem: You're spending too much time in the car.

Solutions:

- If you've been eating in your car, stop.

- Consolidate your errands and plan your routes to make them as short as possible.
- Consider whether your family should cut down on the number of outside activities in which it participates.

- Arrange to participate in carpools so that other people shuttle your family members some of the time.
- Encourage your children—and yourself—to walk or bicycle to activities if that's feasible.
- Designate one day of the week when you won't drive anywhere you have a choice not to go.

Problem: Something in your schedule never gets done.

Solutions:

- Consider whether the item is superfluous, and if it is, then eliminate it from your schedule. If it's really never getting done, then it may not be important. If it really is important, then eliminate something less important so you can get the important item done.
- If it's something no one in the family enjoys doing and someone else can do it, then hire someone to do it.
- Try scheduling it on a different day of the week or at a different time during the day and see whether the change helps. You may have to try several times before finding one that suits your family's rhythm.

Problem: Your family is still scheduling conflicting events.

Solutions:

- If the reason for the conflicting schedules is that your family members aren't entering events in the planner so that other members know not to schedule something at that time, then try to get everyone to understand the importance of using the planner. You can insist that only events entered on the planner will be honored, but a less harsh approach is to ask the master scheduler to check with everyone on a daily basis to see whether new events need to be added to the family's schedule. Chances are, after a few weeks all of your family members will begin using the planner themselves. You can encourage this change in behavior by offering a small reward for any event entered in the planner before the master scheduler has to ask about it.
- If you're allowing your family to overschedule by choosing activities without regard for everyone else's activities, then you need to establish a procedure that requires all family members to check for conflicts before making their own plans. Consider having the whole family collaborate on major decisions such as family parties or the distribution of everyone's enrichment activities.

Problem: Your family's schedule used to work, but now it doesn't.

Solutions:

- Perhaps your family's circumstances have changed—a new job, more home-work, and so on—but you haven't changed the family's schedule. Take some time to reevaluate your family's current circumstances and adjust its schedule accordingly.

- Schedules are always subject to "activity creep." Little by little you add a task here and an activity there, and soon all of the slack in the schedule has been used up and the schedule is overfilled. Ideally, you'll reevaluate your schedule every time you add something new to it. In reality, you'll probably add a certain number of items without any conscious evaluation. The best solution is to enter in your planner a task to analyze your schedule every three months.

Problem: Some days go really well, and others don't.

Solutions:

- If you've broken down your week so that each day has a focus—errands, family time, projects, and so on—check whether it's always the day with the same focus that is giving you trouble. If it is, then work to revamp the way you handle the recurring items on that day.

- If the trouble seems to be more random, look at whether you're having daily chores rotate among your family members. You may discover that one person really likes to walk the dog or do the dishes, whereas another person doesn't. So, on the days when people are happy with the tasks they've been assigned, everything goes smoothly, but on the days when the tasks don't appeal to the people doing them, then the system breaks down. If you can determine who's doing what on the days that work well, then make that set of assignments standard. There's no reason you have to rotate chores among family members if everyone is happy with doing the same set of tasks every day. Do keep in mind that after a while the repetition may lead to boredom, and then you may want to make a temporary—or permanent—change.

- Certain activities in the schedule may just put someone in a contrary mood. For example, a child who truly dislikes piano lessons may end up ruining the schedule for the whole day. Weigh the benefits of the offending activity to the participant against the costs to the whole family.

Chapter Summary

In this chapter, you saw many of the subtleties that go into creating the ultimate family schedule. It isn't rocket science, but it does require a conscious analysis of how your family's required tasks and optional activities mesh with the abilities, interests, personalities, and rhythms of your family members individually and collectively.

You can use the following checklist to make sure that you've fine-tuned your family's schedule as much as possible.

- ❏ Consider family members' body clocks, environmental preferences, and personalities when creating their schedules.
- ❏ Suspend the family's regular schedule when major events warrant it.
- ❏ Modify your planner system if a change will improve its use.
- ❏ Adjust the family's schedule if it isn't running as smoothly as you would like.

We would like to conclude by reminding you that your family's planning tools and schedule need to change over time as your family grows and changes. You would be wise to plan periodically to sit and contemplate how your family's schedule is working and to tweak it slightly or revamp it significantly as your circumstances indicate. Throughout your family's life, new scheduling challenges will always arise, but now you're equipped to meet those challenges, to analyze your options, and to organize your family's schedule in no time.

Day-Timer

Personal organizers, calendars, and planners
Website: www.daytimer.com

Filofax

Personal organizers
Website: www.filofaxusa.com

Franklin Covey

Personal planners
Website: www.franklincovey.com

If you're looking for a dry-erase or magnetic planner, Flex-A-Chart Manufacturing offers a wide selection:

Flex-A-Chart Manufacturing

Wipe-off and magnetic calendars and accessories
Website: www.flex-a-chart.com

The following two companies are listed here because we mentioned their unique planners in this book and they're not available in retail stores:

Sidetracked Home Executives (SHE)

Personal planner
Website: www.shesintouch.com

FlyLady and Company, Inc.

Family wall calendar
Website: www.flylady.net

Part IV

Appendixes

Product Resources

This appendix is designed to provide you with an easy reference of websites and other locations where you can find both the specific products mentioned throughout this book and other products like them.

Planner Systems

The backbone of your organized family schedule is the group planner system you select, together with the individual planners that your family members choose. Here, we've summarized many of the commercial options available to you.

Hard-Copy Planners

Several companies manufacture hard-copy planners. If you're looking for one that's paper-based, you may want to compare the different configurations available through the following companies:

AT-A-GLANCE

Calendars and planners

Website: www.ataglance.com

Day Runner

Planners and organizers

Website: www.dayrunner.com

Electronic Planners

Electronic planners use software that runs using the planner's operating system. If you have an electronic planner with one operating system, then it won't be compatible with another planner or software that uses a different operating system. Here, we've listed the major PDA operating systems as well as a couple of products that use their own proprietary software:

BlackBerry

Wireless handheld technology
Website: www.blackberry.com

K-Group Industries

Handheld organizers for children
Website: www.kgiproducts.com

PalmOne

PDAs and smartphones
Website: www.palmone.com

Windows Mobile

Windows mobile-based pocket PCs
Website: www.microsoft.com/windowsmobile/pocketpc/ppc/default.mspx

Simpliciti, Inc.

Multiuser electronic planner
Website: www.simpliciti.com

Symbian

Symbian OS for data-enabled mobile phones
Website: www.symbian.com

Hybrid System

If you want to record information using pen and paper but want to retrieve or share the information electronically using the Windows operating system, check out the following:

Logitech io2 Digital Writing System

Website: www.logitech.com

Scheduling Software

Many calendar and scheduling software programs are available. The following is a list of the ones we've referenced throughout the book:

NetSimplicity Family Scheduler

Operating system: Windows
Website: www.netsimplicity.com

Calendars Net

Online calendar hosting
Website: www.calendars.net

Collabrio MyEvents

Online calendar, contact manager, and task lists
Website: www.myevents.com

Dr. State's Computer Parent Family Software

Operating system: Windows
Website: www.computerparent.com

PDAsoftnet Student Log V 1.0

Operating system: Palm OS
Website: www.pdasoftnet.com

Retailers

Although we've listed product-specific websites throughout the book, most of the products are available through retailers, as well. You can find a lot of information about the products on their manufacturers' websites, but you may find that shopping at a retailer is more convenient—and often less expensive—than dealing directly with the manufacturer.

Planners and Supplies

Almost all of the calendars, planners, accessories, and office supplies we've mentioned throughout the book are available—usually at a discount—through one or more of the major office supply retail chains:

Office Depot

Website: www.officedepot.com

OfficeMax

Website: www.officemax.com

Reliable Office Supplies

Website: www.reliable.com

Staples

Website: www.staples.com

Viking Office Products

Website: www.vikingop.com

Many of the electronic products are also available through

Amazon.com

Website: www.amazon.com

Specialty Organizing Products

In addition to the websites we've noted throughout the book for specific products, most of the specialized organizing products can be purchased through

OnlineOrganizing.com

Website: www.onlineorganizing.com

The medication reminders are available through

e-pill Medication Reminders

Website: www.epill.com

A few of the products are more difficult to find, so we've relisted them here along with their manufacturers' or suppliers' websites for your convenience:

AT-A-GLANCE Four-Person Daily Group Appointment Book
At-A-GLANCE Eight-Person Daily Group Appointment Book

Website: www.ataglance.com

Trend Enterprises, Inc. chore charts

Website: www.trendenterprises.com

Franklin Covey Middle School Planner

Website: www.franklincovey.com

KeyRinger remote control locator

Website: www.keyringer.com

"The Ultimate College Checklist" booklet by Diana Zimmerman

Website: www.solutions4organizing.com

PRO TEC International musical instrument cases

Website: www.ptcases.com

Wilson Sporting Goods sports equipment bags

Website: www.wilson.com

Coghlan Dynalite flashlight

Website: www.coghlans.com

Swivel Car Seat

Website: www.aidsforarthritis.com

General Motors Sit-and-Lift Power Seat

Website: www.gmmobility.com

Professional Organizing Services

If you would like personalized help setting up your family's planner system and schedule, then you may want to engage the services of a professional organizer. Here is a list of associations that can assist you with finding the right professional organizer for your needs:

NAPO—The National Association of Professional Organizers, now in its 20th year, is The Organizing Authority with more than 2,700 members, mostly in the United States, but also in Canada and seven other countries. The organization has an online automated referral system to help you locate the right organizer in your geographical area.
Website: www.napo.net

NSGCD—The National Study Group on Chronic Disorganization will refer you to a professional organizer who specializes in working with chronically disorganized clients, people who have struggled with staying organized all of their lives.
Website: www.nsgcd.org

POC—Professional Organizers in Canada is entering its 6th year, with more than 200 members, mostly across Canada. The organization has an online automated referral system to help you locate the right organizer in your geographical area.
Website: www.organizersincanada.com

Reading References

If you would like to learn more details about some of the topics that were touched on only briefly in this book because they weren't our main focus, this appendix provides you with a list of references.

Articles

"Choosing a Pet"
http://la.essortment.com/choosingpets_rudb.htm

"Music Training and the Brain"
http://web.sfn.org/content/Publications/
BrainBriefings/music_training_and_brain.htm

"Sorry, Kids, Piano Lessons Make You Smarter" by E.J. Mundell for HealthDayNews
http://www.forbes.com/lifestyle/2004/07/15/
cx_0715health.html

"Piano Lessons Found to Enhance Reasoning" by Debra Viadero
http://www.edweek.org/ew/vol-16/24brain.h16

"Selecting a Geriatric Care Manager"
http://www.ftc.gov/bcp/conline/pubs/services/apact/
apact08.htm

"Caring for the Caregiver"
http://www.ftc.gov/bcp/conline/pubs/services/apact/
apact09.htm

"Are You a Lark, an Owl, or a Hummingbird?"
http://nasw.org/users/llamberg/larkowl.htm

"Dehydration; A Hidden Source of Fatigue" by Gordon Dupont
`http://www.evergreenairlines.com/safety_new/html/articles_med/med0005.html`

Books

Barmeier, Jim. *The Brain.* San Diego: Lucent Books, 1996.

Beerman, Susan, and Judith Rappaport-Musson. *Eldercare 911: The Caregiver's Complete Handbook for Making Decisions.* Amherst, NY: Prometheus Books, 2002.

Farenga, Patrick. *The Beginner's Guide to Homeschooling.* Cambridge, MA: Holt Associates/GWS, 2000.

Maas, James B. *Power Sleep.* New York: Villard Books, 1998.

Saba, Laura, and Julie Gattis. *The McGraw-Hill Homeschooling Companion.* New York: McGraw-Hill, 2002.

Tobias, Cynthia Ulrich. *The Way We Work: What You Know About Working Styles Can Increase Your Efficiency, Productivity, and Job Satisfaction.* Nashville: Broadman & Holman, 1995.

Websites

www.enchantedlearning.com/graphicorganizers

EnchantedLearning.com. On this particular page of this user-supported website, you can learn about various types of activity maps (graphic organizers).

www.sleepfoundation.org

The National Sleep Foundation. This site contains up-to-date information on sleep research.

www.aspca.org

The American Society for the Prevention of Cruelty to Animals. This site includes information about pet ownership.

www.collegeboard.com

CollegeBoard. From the company that brings us the standardized SAT and AP tests, this site also contains helpful information for college-bound students.

www.commonapp.org

The Common Application. This site contains the recommended form of 255 selective colleges and universities for admission to their undergraduate programs.

www.fastweb.com

FastWeb. This site provides free scholarship and college search features.

www.mowaa.org

Meals on Wheels Association of America. This site has an automated feature so you can find a Meals on Wheels provider in your area.

www.n4a.org

National Association of Area Agencies on Aging. Your Area Agency on Aging can provide information on many eldercare issues.

www.caremanager.org

National Association of Professional Geriatric Care Managers. This site has an automated referral feature to help you find a geriatric care manager in your area.

Index

driving

commutes, scheduling, 189

drivers, scheduling, 122-123

drivers education, scheduling, 176-177

eldercare transportation services, 204

Sit-and-Lift Power Seats (General Motors), 199

Swivel Car Seats, 198

teenagers, scheduling, 176-178

vehicle maintenance, 133

E

effectiveness of schedules, 78-79

efficiency schedules

automatic watering systems, 82-83

grocery lists, 80-81

portable offices, 84

time-saving gadgets, 81-82

eldercare

adult day care, 205

appointments, scheduling, 197-198

assisted living facilities, 205

caregiver respites, scheduling, 205

common tasks, consolidating, 196

emergency preparations, 203-204

family schedules, accommodating into, 195-197

geriatric care managers, 205

housekeeping, 204

in-home services, 204

insurance claims, submitting, 202-203

meals, 204

medical situations, managing, 197-204

medications, tracking, 198-202

needs, determining, 194-195

Sit-and-Lift Power Seats (General Motors), 199

Swivel Car Seats, 198

electronic planners

accessibility, 14-16

backups, 38-39

checklist integration, 93-94

children, 166-167

choosing, 18-24, 166-167, 188

comparing, 16, 24-25

cost comparisions, 24-25

ergonomics, 36

events, scheduling, 37

features of, 13, 18

locating, 36

managing, 40-44

multiuser planning devices, 36

online, 15

Palm OS, 39

PDA, 16

schedules, printing, 37

shared desktop computers, 36

Simpliciti Home Organizers, 16

software, 38-39, 181

Student Log V 1.0 (PDAsoftnet), 181

teenagers, 180-181

Looking for professional organizing assistance?

Contact the Organizing Authority!

 **The National Association of Professional Organizers**

Whether you need to organize your business or your home, NAPO members are ready to help you meet the challenge.

A professional organizer enhances the lives of clients by designing systems and processes using organizing principles and through transferring organizing skills. A professional organizer also educates the public on organizing solutions and the resulting benefits.

NAPO currently has more than 2,700 members throughout the U.S. and in 8 other countries ready to serve you.

For More Information or to Find a Professional Organizer in Your Area,

Visit the NAPO Web Site at **www.NAPO.net.**

Do Even More
...In No Time

Must See

Get ready to cross off those items on your to-do list! *In No Time* helps you tackle the projects that you don't think you have time to finish. With shopping lists and step-by-step instructions, these books get you working toward accomplishing your goals.

Check out these other *In No Time* books, coming soon!

Start Your Own Home Business In No Time
ISBN: **0-7897-3224-6**
$16.95
September 2004

Plan a Fabulous Party In No Time
ISBN: **0-7897-3221-1**
$16.95
November 2004

Speak Basic Spanish In No Time
ISBN: **0-7897-3223-8**
$16.95
October 2004

Organize Your Garage In No Time
ISBN: **0-7897-3219-X**
$16.95
February 2005

Quick Family Meals In No Time
ISBN: **0-7897-3299-8**
$16.95
October 2004

Organize Your Personal Finances In No Time
ISBN: **0-7897-3179-7**
$16.95
August 2004